RECIPES FROM A KITCHEN GARDEN

RECIPES FROM A KITCHEN GARDEN

Renee Shepherd and Fran Raboff

Ten Speed Press
Berkeley, California

🖐️

TEN SPEED PRESS
P.O. Box 7123
Berkeley, CA 94707

Cover design by Fifth Street Design
Text design by Linda Lane, Woodland Graphics

Library of Congress Cataloging-in-Publication Data
Shepherd, Renee.
Recipes from a kitchen garden / Renee Shepherd and Fran Raboff.
p.   cm.
Originally published in 2 vol.: 1st ed. Felton, Calif. :
Shepherd's Garden Pub., c1987-c1991.
Includes index.
ISBN 0-89815-540-1
1. Cookery (Vegetables)   I. Raboff, Fran.   II. Title.
TX801.S49 1993
641.6'5—dc20   93-16018
                                                  CIP

FIRST PRINTING 1993

Printed in Canada

2   3   4   5   6   —   99   98   97   96   95

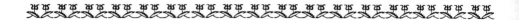

DEDICATION

To my sister Susan and brother-in-law Bill,
with love and gratitude
for their support, safe haven,
and all the laughter and adventures we've shared.

CONTENTS

ACKNOWLEDGMENTS

Linda Lane's graphic skills lend a very special grace and sensitivity to all our joint creative projects. Her innate good humor and professionalism have been central in seeing them through to completion.

Mimi Osborne's exceptional talent as an illustrator is obvious to everyone who reads this book. Her attention to detail and meticulous rendering combine with a sophisticated knowledge of horticulture to make her a marvelous partner.

Dotty Hollinger has translated my handwritten scrawl into expertly typed copy with kindness, patience and calm efficiency, a task I still feel is miraculous even after fifteen years of projects as diverse as my Ph.D. thesis, reams of catalog copy, essays, recipes, seed packet backs and now this cookbook.

Accomplished author Rosalind Creasy has given needed advice and direction ever since I began to share my love for growing and cooking. Her keen intellect, resourcefulness and wonderful personality have been a blessing of friendship for many years.

The gentle spirit of coworker and friend Beth Benjamin enhances everything I do. She is the keeper of Alan Chadwick's light, fellow garden lover, resident flower expert, idea generator, research partner, office manager and the chief mainstay in keeping the seed business on track, enabling me to finish this book.

Wendy Krupnick's clear and committed horticultural vision, gardening expertise and boundless energy make the gardens bountiful and meaningful for me.

David Pearce's wit and insight have helped me through the inevitable writer's block and the occasional doldrums of everyday life and he skillfully keeps everything up and running smoothly in my gardens and household.

Glenna von Gease keeps my working life organized and on schedule; a far cry from the hours riding our horses through the redwoods years ago, but a wonderful testimony to the joys of working with true friends.

Happy and loving thanks go to Al Raboff for his good humor, discerning tastebuds and endless enthusiasm during the dozens of tasting and testing sessions.

Finally, thank you to all the wonderful seed catalog customers and many friends whose visits, letters, comments and interest underscored and inspired the entire process of creating this cookbook.

DEAR FRIENDS,

My kitchen garden is a classic example of the chicken-and-egg puzzle: I really can't say if I began gardening to have the freshest, best-tasting vegetables to cook with, or if I became more interested in cooking once I had a garden of bountiful and abundant produce. Probably both are true, because growing fresh vegetables and herbs finds its natural completion in preparing them well. Good cooks nationwide have begun to focus on dishes that feature fresh local vegetables and herbs, and many fine restaurants have produce grown for them by small market gardeners. But it is really your own garden that can consistently provide the full-flavored fresh ingredients necessary for this healthy and appetizing style of cooking and eating at home. Put in another way, in an age of supermarkets and square tomatoes, we must become our own greengrocers!

FROM GARDEN TO KITCHEN

The seed catalog I began features vegetable, herb and edible-flower seeds selected and bred for tenderness and flavor, including a wide range of fine European varieties and the best domestic seeds. To help our customers enjoy what they grow, the catalog also includes as many good recipes as we can fit in. I have also found that while it is one thing to prepare a store-bought vegetable three or four times a month, it is quite another challenge to find interesting ways of using that big rush of ripe zucchini, steady daily harvest of tomatoes and green beans, or the first basket of less familiar vegetables like chiles or fennel. While having an abundance of fresh basil is a luxury, every basil lover appreciates a change from weeks of pesto sauce. This cookbook is a collection of our recipes, designed to give both the cooking gardener and wise shopper an array of satisfying ways of using fresh-picked, first-rate vegetables and herbs to produce good food on a daily basis. You'll find all these recipes can be made in a reasonable amount of time by today's busy cooks. Our recipes are not novel or extreme, but rely on a style that gives priority to flavor and presentation without using exotic or hard-to-find ingredients. They are a new compilation of the two smaller volumes we have offered in our catalog over the last eight years.

HOW OUR GARDEN GROWS

I began gardening fifteen years ago in my backyard with a series first of sixteen, then twenty-four 4 × 20-foot boxed raised beds, gardened organically in the French Intensive manner. The garden now also includes a considerable collection of pots and containers on my back deck so we can understand the

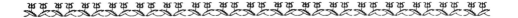

needs and desires of small-space gardeners. Another large one-half-acre garden is next to the horse pasture in the lower field (where we used to play soccer in pre-seed-catalog days). This big lower garden is laid out in a series of long raised beds. Most of the hot-weather and space lovers such as tomatoes, squash, melons, peppers, eggplants and sun-worshipping flowers have been moved to its sunny location. The original raised-bed backyard garden next to the house still grows all the leafy greens, herbs and brassicas and now includes a permanent herb garden. The herb beds reflect my own fascination with different kinds of basils and edible flowers, and interest in having a continuous supply of many different fresh culinary herbs throughout the gardening seasons. The herb garden also enables us to enjoy the sense of historical continuity provided by centuries-old traditions of herbal lore.

My gardens serve three purposes. They are demonstration and "living catalog" gardens for visitors who come to see and sample the varieties currently offered in our seed catalog; kitchen gardens whose produce we enjoy and develop recipes from; and trial gardens for our two-year evaluations of new varieties. One section of the demonstration garden is always devoted to our specialty basils, since everyone who comes by looks forward to seeing, tasting and smelling them. I love the colors, textures and flavors of a wide variety of salad plants, so there are usually nine or ten small plantings of different lettuces and other salads in spring and fall, and five or six heat-tolerant varieties in summer. In the big lower garden, we always have a section dedicated to our search for new, flavorful and early-bearing tomatoes—plants whose seeds came with high promise from Italy, England, France and Japan, as well as several American heirloom favorites to taste and compare. These three functions of trial garden, demonstration garden and working kitchen garden sometimes produce unique dilemmas. For example, we are often faced with the need to harvest all the cinnamon or lemon basil for a recipe-testing session the very same week a visiting group is coming especially to see the very same herbs in the scented-basil garden. These challenges keep things interesting all season long.

As the seed catalog business has grown and I do more traveling both in this country and throughout Europe to find new seeds and cooking ideas, my job as head gardener has inevitably taken on new partners. I now plan and organize the gardens with Wendy Krupnick, a dedicated and experienced master gardener and longtime secretary of the California Certified Organic Growers.

The trial gardens continue to expand annually as I locate new varieties, talk with restaurant folks and visit our home garden customers and gourmet specialty growers. When touring the trials of new cultivars at traditional commercial breeders, I find I am still the only one who actually tastes selections as

well as evaluates their cultural attributes. (Most commercial seed buyers are interested only in such qualities as uniformity, earliness, etc.) I also actively seek out heirloom vegetables and flowers that may have been preserved in individual gardens or in certain regions of the country for years, but have been neglected or discontinued by the commercial trade.

COOKING FRENZY, OR HOW WE DEVELOP THESE RECIPES

Each spring, cooking partner Fran Raboff and I sit down with a list of vegetables, herbs and flowers, a huge pile of customers' and chefs' recipe suggestions, and all the cooking articles and ideas we've saved all year. Two times a week for the next four months we get together for planning, discussion and cooking sessions with the goal of having a complete set of finished new recipes for every vegetable and herb each season.

Our cooking sessions begin early in the morning, when Fran does the shopping for that day's seven or eight new dishes and Wendy picks the fresh produce we need from the garden. In the afternoon I arrive (usually late, I must admit), feeling much blessed to emerge from our busy office into Fran's large, light and beautifully appointed kitchen. I bring along all the vegetables and herbs Wendy harvested from the garden. Fran and I then work our way through the new dishes, changing, testing and inventing as we go. Finally, when all is ready, Fran's husband Al (a truly generous bon vivant and, by the way, a master craftsman of beautiful wooden toys) and invited friends join us for a long and enjoyable testing meal. We have our dinners at their commodious kitchen table overlooking a beautiful view of the grassy and forested hills that surround their mountain retirement home.

As we taste and comment, I keep a stack of the penciled recipes by my side, noting everyone's comments and reactions to each dish. Often Fran or I spring up from the table to see, for example, if the flavor of a salad dressing needs a bit more lemon juice or if a bean dish might be better with a bit of tarragon or a touch more scallion, as everyone gives their suggestions and opinions on how things go together.

Each session produces winners—recipes to retest and probably use—as well as losers (although we always learn something about flavor combinations even on dishes that don't seem special enough to repeat). Then comes the more tedious process of retesting and writing up and checking to make sure everything is just right. Much of the success of this process is due to Fran's creative skills. She is, first and foremost, an artist and accomplished sculptor, and having her talents applied to recipe development always expands my cooking horizons.

What We Consider

In creating these recipes, we keep in mind that our readers, like ourselves, are seeking delicious, easy-to-prepare dishes that emphasize fresh ingredients. We try to avoid rich sauces while maximizing simplicity of style, wonderful flavors and appetizing presentation. Happily, these goals are easy for fellow home gardeners to achieve. Being our own greengrocers, we can cook with what is in season at its flavorful best, emphasizing the true honest flavors of tender produce. We also work with our freshly picked herbs to provide subtle flavor accents and succulent fragrance to our dishes. It's especially interesting to make edible flower and herb blossom recipes because, although traditions of flower cookery are long and ancient, there is a shortage of modern flower recipes that taste as good as they look.

Finally

All the recipes in this cookbook have been served with pride and pleasure to my family and friends in many satisfying and memorable meals over the last several seasons. I invite you to enjoy them with us. Please continue to send me your feedback and ideas. I look forward to continuing these written conversations, for they are one of the biggest rewards that have grown from my original impulse to share my own enthusiasm and love for the inner and outer joys of cooking from the garden.

Renee Shepherd

VEGETABLES

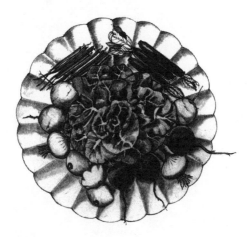

*F*resh vegetables have their very own special allure, and these recipes are first and foremost a celebration of their ingredients. The sweet perfume of a perfectly ripe melon, the silky sheen of deep purple eggplants, the glorious red of summer tomatoes and the lacy greens and bronzes of lush lettuce rosettes both please the eye and delight the spirit of the gardening cook. Bringing this beautiful abundance into the kitchen presents the delightful challenge of creating dishes to emphasize and enhance the flavors, colors and textures of the harvest. Beauty, freshness and full flavor are our raw materials and these finished dishes are offered in hopes that you will find both satisfaction and joy in their preparation and savor in eating them with your family and friends.

BEANS

JANICE'S PICKLED BASIL BEANS

These crispy, basil-scented beans are a fine appetizer or satisfying between-meal nibble. One of our favorite ways to utilize a bean harvest.

**3 to 4 pounds fresh green snap
   beans, rinsed
5 cups mild white vinegar
5 cups water (not softened water)
1 tablespoon sugar
¼ cup pickling salt**

**FOR EACH JAR:
4 peppercorns
2 cloves garlic, peeled
4 to 6 large fresh basil leaves**

Wash 8 pint or 4 quart canning jars with hot soapy water and rinse, or run them through the dishwasher.

Trim the ends of the beans. Bring to a boil the vinegar, water, sugar and salt.

In the bottom of each jar, put the peppercorns, garlic cloves and basil leaves, then pack them with beans, leaving ½ inch headspace. Fill the jars with the hot brine, leaving ½ inch. Wipe the jar rims and seal. Process 15 minutes in a boiling water bath (20 minutes for quarts). Wait about 4 weeks before opening to let the flavors blend and deepen.

Makes 4 quarts

GREEN BEANS À L'ANGLAISE

This is how fine restaurants prepare fresh beans.

Take fresh beans, a large pot of water, and 1 or 2 tablespoons of salt. (The salt sets the green color and you rinse it off in the cold running water.) Bring salted water to a rolling boil, put in the trimmed beans and cook until just tender-crisp. Drain beans into a colander and cool immediately under very cold running water. Drain on paper or kitchen towels. The beans will be a beautiful dark green. Use in salads, or reheat the beans thoroughly in some butter with fresh herbs just before serving.

Green Bean and Red Bell Pepper Vinaigrette

2 cups fresh green beans, trimmed
   and blanched
2 red bell peppers, thinly sliced
½ teaspoon chopped scallions
⅓ cup sherry wine vinegar
pinch sugar
2 tablespoons water
salt and pepper to taste
½ cup vegetable oil

Toss all the above ingredients together and chill one hour before serving to blend the flavors.

Serves 4

Green Beans with Mushrooms

½ onion, finely chopped
2 tablespoons butter
½ pound mushrooms, thickly
   sliced
1 pound green beans, trimmed
   and cut into 2-inch lengths
1 cup chicken stock
½ teaspoon paprika
¼ teaspoon dill
salt and pepper to taste
½ cup sour cream

Brown the onions in the butter. Add the mushrooms and fry about 2 minutes, stirring occasionally. Remove from heat. Blanch the beans in salted water for about 30 seconds. Drain. Add the chicken stock to the mushrooms and onions. Bring to a boil. Add the paprika, dill, and salt and pepper to taste. Boil for 5 minutes. Add the green beans and sour cream. Simmer at very low heat for 10 minutes and serve.

Serves 4

Fresh Bean Salad Anglaise

1 cup each of yellow and green
   snap beans, cooked à l'Anglaise
   (see page 3)

DRESSING:
6 small scallions, finely
   chopped
2 tablespoons tarragon vinegar,
   or your favorite herbed
   vinegar
1 teaspoon salt
2 teaspoons Dijon mustard
½ cup olive oil

GARNISH:
chopped parsley or chives

Whisk together scallions, vinegar, salt and mustard; add oil and whisk to blend well. Let dressing stand until ready to use. Put well-drained beans in a serving bowl. Just before serving the beans, stir dressing again and pour it over them. Toss lightly to blend. Sprinkle with chopped parsley or chives for a nice accent.

Serves 4

Green Bean Pâté with Basil

This dish tastes sinfully rich, but it's not in the least, so enjoy!

> ½ pound fresh green beans, trimmed
> 1 tablespoon vegetable oil
> 1 onion, coarsely chopped
> 3 hard-boiled eggs
> 3 tablespoons finely chopped fresh basil
> 1 teaspoon lemon rind
> lowfat mayonnaise
> seasoned salt and pepper to taste
> melba toast or crackers

> GARNISH:
> nasturtium flowers

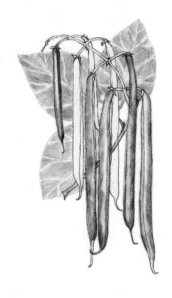

Cook beans until tender by boiling or steaming them. In a skillet, heat oil; add onion and sauté until softened. Cool. In a food processor or with a food chopper, process or grind green beans, onions, eggs, basil and lemon rind until roughly puréed. Remove to a bowl; mix in just enough mayonnaise to hold mixture together. Stir in seasoned salt and pepper to taste. Chill. Garnish with whole nasturtium blossoms. Serve with melba toast or crackers.

Makes 2 cups

Green Beans with Pecans

> 1½ pounds green beans, trimmed
> 1 tablespoon olive oil
> 2 tablespoons butter
> ¼ cup chopped scallions or shallots
> ¼ cup chopped fresh parsley
> 1 cup pecan pieces, toasted
> salt and white pepper to taste
> optional: 1 to 2 teaspoons chopped fresh summer savory or ½ teaspoon dried

Cook the beans until just tender. Meanwhile, heat oil and butter in a pan and sauté the scallions or shallots until softened. Stir in the parsley (and savory if used) and blend. Add the beans and pecans, season with salt and pepper—toss and serve.

Serves 6

Chilled Green Beans with Creamy Horseradish Dressing

Especially good served as a salad with thick slices of tomatoes.

To serve 4 to 6 people, cook enough slender green beans in salted water until just tender-crisp. Refresh beans with ice water to stop the cooking, drain, pat dry and refrigerate.

Mix together 1 tablespoon horseradish, ½ teaspoon Dijon mustard, 2 tablespoons vegetable oil, ⅓ cup sour cream, salt and white pepper to taste. Chill one hour.

Lay the beans on a big serving plate and spoon sauce over them. Serve immediately.

Green Beans in Basil-Walnut Vinaigrette

For a lovely presentation, put 1 to 2 radicchio or red cabbage leaves on each salad plate and mound the green beans on top.

1½ pounds young green beans, trimmed

VINAIGRETTE:
1 teaspoon chopped garlic
20 basil leaves
½ teaspoon salt
½ teaspoon freshly ground pepper
2 teaspoons Dijon mustard
4 tablespoons white wine vinegar
½ cup olive oil

GARNISH:
chopped walnuts
3 scallions, thinly sliced

Bring a large pot of salted water to a rolling boil, add green beans and cook until just tender-crisp, 3 to 5 minutes. Drain immediately into a colander and pour ice water over beans to stop the cooking action. Drain well.

In a blender or food processor put the garlic, basil, salt and ground pepper. Pulse on and off, then add the mustard and vinegar. Pulse until smooth. Add the oil very slowly in a thin stream with the machine running, just until blended.

Place the beans in a serving bowl and pour the vinaigrette over them. Toss to coat thoroughly. Garnish with the scallions and walnuts.

Serves 6 to 8

GINGERED GREEN BEANS

The piquant flavor of ginger is a natural complement to the taste of fresh beans.

> 1 tablespoon butter (or 1 teaspoon butter and 2 teaspoons oil)
> 1 small onion, very thinly sliced
> 2 teaspoons finely chopped fresh ginger
> ¼ teaspoon crushed fennel seed
> ¼ teaspoon salt
> 1 pound haricots verts or young green beans, trimmed and cut into ½-inch pieces
> ¼ cup chicken stock

Heat butter in a large skillet. Add the onion, ginger, fennel seed and salt. Sauté until onions are glazed and translucent. Add beans and stock. Cover and cook only until beans are tender-crisp.

Serves 4 to 6

PIA'S ITALIAN COUNTRY BEANS

Another dish that tastes rich without actually being so.

> 3 tablespoons olive oil
> 2 cloves garlic, minced
> 1 pound green beans, trimmed
> 1 cup beef stock
> 1 tablespoon finely chopped fresh parsley,
> ¼ cup finely chopped ham or prosciutto

Heat oil and sauté garlic until it becomes fragrant—2 to 3 minutes. Add green beans and sauté 2 to 3 minutes until glossy and well coated. Add stock, cover and cook until beans are just tender-crisp. Sprinkle with chopped parsley and ham, and serve.

Serves 4 to 6

GREEN BEANS WITH TARRAGON

The peppery/anise taste of fresh tarragon pairs beautifully with the vivid flavor of fresh green beans.

> 1 pound green beans, trimmed
> 1 tablespoon olive oil
> 1 tablespoon butter
> 1 small clove garlic, minced
> 3 tablespoons finely chopped scallions
> ⅓ cup thinly sliced celery
> 2 tablespoons finely chopped fresh tarragon or 2 teaspoons dried
> salt and freshly ground pepper to taste

Bring a large pot of salted water to a boil. Put in green beans and cook until just tender-crisp, 3 to 5 minutes. Drain beans in a colander and plunge immediately into ice water to stop the cooking action. Drain on paper towels. Cut beans into 1-inch pieces. Set aside. Heat olive oil and butter in a large skillet. Add garlic, scallions and celery and sauté until softened. Add beans and tarragon; sauté until heated through. Season with salt and fresh pepper to taste.

Serves 4 to 6

Baby Green Beans with Roasted Garlic, Anchovies, Olive Oil and Almonds

2 pounds baby green beans
1 large bulb garlic, roasted*
1 two-ounce can anchovies,
  drained and chopped
½ to ¾ cup almond halves
½ cup olive oil
2 tablespoons red wine vinegar
1 teaspoon Worcestershire sauce

GARNISH:
whole lettuce leaves
red pepper strips

Lightly blanch beans—cook just until tender-crisp. Cool quickly by plunging into cold water to stop cooking action. Drain and set aside.

Squeeze the roasted garlic pulp from the cloves. Combine the roasted garlic pulp with the anchovies, almonds, olive oil, vinegar and Worcestershire sauce and mix together. Toss with the drained beans and allow to sit at room temperature for an hour before serving to blend the flavors.

Serve on lettuce and garnish with red pepper strips.

Serves 6

To roast garlic: Cut off the top half-inch of the bulb with a serrated knife. Rub the outside of the bulb and the cut surfaces with olive oil. Bake at 375°F for about 25 to 35 minutes until the cloves, when pierced with a fork, have a very soft consistency, like butter. When garlic is soft, cool the bulb and then squeeze the roasted garlic pulp from the individual cloves.

BEETS

DUTCH BEET SALAD

6 large beets, peeled
1 bunch scallions, chopped
½ cup apple cider vinegar
2 tablespoons water
½ cup vegetable oil
pinch sugar
¼ teaspoon salt
¼ teaspoon black pepper

Grate the fresh beets on the finest grater you have—preferably one used to grate lemon peel. If you are using a food processor, use the blade with the smallest holes. Place the grated beets in a bowl. Mix the remaining ingredients until blended and pour over the beets. Toss and marinate in refrigerator for several hours before serving. For an interesting variation substitute grated carrots and/or grated daikon radishes for one-third of the beets.

Serves 4 to 6

BAKED BEETS

Once you have cooked red beets in this manner, you won't ever boil them again. In France they cook the beets before they come to market, and they are wonderful. Just pull up your beets, cut the tops back to about 3 inches, brush off most of the dirt and put the beets on aluminum foil on a cookie sheet. Bake in a 375°F oven for approximately 1 hour—or until a fork pierces the beets easily. Remove from oven, cool, and remove the skins (and remaining tops). Now the beets can be prepared in any style—buttered, Harvard, pickled, etc. We love them just simply buttered. The flavor after baking is intensified and delicious.

Romanian Summer Soup

For a hot summer day or evening. The soup is as flavorful as it is beautiful. For a change, try this with our golden beets. Serve chilled or at room temperature with thick slices of pumpernickel or fresh rye bread and butter.

> 6 medium beets, including tops
> 2 medium onions
> 8 cups chicken stock
> 1 cup sour cream
> 1 cup plain fresh yogurt
> 2 cucumbers, peeled and coarsely chopped
> 1 bunch radishes, thinly sliced
> 1 tablespoon lemon juice
> salt and pepper to taste
> 1 or 2 tablespoons chopped fresh dill or 1 tablespoon dried

Peel the beets and cut into julienne strips. Wash and coarsely chop the beet greens and chop the onions. In a large pot, heat the chicken stock and add the beets, beet greens and onions. Cook covered until the beets are tender, about 20 minutes. Remove from heat. Cool to room temperature, and then stir in the sour cream and yogurt. Add the chopped cucumber, radishes and the lemon juice. Correct seasoning, adding salt and pepper to taste. Serve in individual bowls with fresh dill sprinkled on top.

Serves 8

Beet Borscht

Refreshing, beautifully colored and especially good on a very hot day.

> 12 ounces cooked beets
> 1½ cups beef or chicken stock
> zest of 1 lemon (yellow part of peel)
> juice of 1 lemon
> 3 or 4 tablespoons chopped fresh dill
> ½ teaspoon salt
> ¼ teaspoon black pepper
> 6 scallions, chopped
> 2 cups sour cream (or 1 cup sour cream and 1 cup fresh plain yogurt)

> GARNISH:
> chopped chives
> chive blossoms

In a blender or food processor combine beets with stock. Add lemon zest and juice, dill, salt, pepper and scallions. Puree until smooth, pour into a bowl and blend in the sour cream. Chill in the refrigerator until very cold. Taste for seasoning; it should be nice and lemony. Top each bowl with another spoonful of sour cream and the chopped chives with their blossoms.

Serves 6

LEMON LOVERS' BEETS

1 lemon
2 tablespoons butter
1 tablespoon sugar
**8 small to medium cooked beets,
  quartered (or use baby beets)**
1 tablespoon chopped parsley

Grate lemon rind and reserve. Squeeze juice. Melt butter in a saucepan and add the sugar and lemon juice. Cook over moderate heat about 5 minutes or until slightly syrupy. Add the cooked beets and heat through, stirring.

Garnish with the lemon rind and chopped parsley and serve.

Serves 2 to 3

PICKLED BABY BEETS AND EGGS

1 pound baby beets, trimmed
1 small onion, very finely sliced
4 to 6 hard-boiled eggs, shelled
2 tablespoons brown sugar
**2 to 3 tablespoons red wine
  vinegar**
4 whole cloves
pinch of salt and pepper

Cook the beets in enough boiling water to cover until they are just tender. Reserve the water and skin the beets. Strain the water to remove any residue, then add the sliced onion and the whole hard-boiled eggs, the brown sugar, vinegar, cloves and a pinch of salt and pepper. Taste and adjust the seasonings.

Marinate for 1 to 4 days in the refrigerator. The deep ruby marinade will become more intense and color the eggs a rosy hue. This dish stores well in the fridge.

Serves 4 to 6

GINGER-ORANGE BEETS

A richly satisfying way to prepare beets that marries several well-matched flavors.

**6 large beets, cooked in their skins
  until almost tender and cooled**
1 large orange
**4 slices bacon, cut into ½-inch
  pieces**
1 medium onion, diced
1 tablespoon grated fresh ginger
2 tablespoons light brown sugar
2 tablespoons raspberry vinegar
½ cup chicken stock
salt and freshly ground pepper
**½ teaspoon cornstarch, dissolved
  in 1 teaspoon water**

Peel and slice beets ¼ to ½ inch thick. Remove the orange zest (orange part of skin only) of the orange. Cut the zest into fine julienne strips. Squeeze the orange—you should have about ½ cup juice. In a deep skillet, cook bacon until golden and almost crisp. Discard most of fat. Add onions and sauté until softened—2 to 3 minutes. Add ginger, brown sugar, orange zest and juice, vinegar and stock and combine. Add beets and cook over low heat for 10 to 15 minutes, stirring frequently. Add salt and pepper to taste. Just before serving, add dissolved cornstarch and water and heat until thickened.

Serves 4

Broccoli

Broccoli Salad

2 heads broccoli, cut into medium
florets with 1-inch stems

DRESSING:
⅓ cup vegetable oil
2 tablespoons chopped sweet
pickle, or pickle relish
2 tablespoons chopped fresh
parsley
2 tablespoons chopped red or
green bell pepper
2 tablespoons white wine vinegar
1 tablespoon chopped fresh
chives
1 tablespoon chopped fresh
tarragon or 1½ teaspoons dried
¾ teaspoon salt
¾ teaspoon sugar
½ clove garlic, minced
pinch of cayenne pepper

GARNISH:
1 hard-boiled egg, chopped
nasturtium and/or calendula
blossoms

Whisk together all dressing ingredients and set aside to let flavors blend. Bring a pot of water to a boil and boil or steam the broccoli until it is tender-crisp—done but not overcooked! Immediately transfer to a bowl of ice water to stop the cooking process and keep the broccoli bright green. Drain and cool in refrigerator until well chilled. Arrange the chilled broccoli on a serving platter and pour over the blended dressing. Garnish with chopped egg and calendula or nasturtium blossoms.

Serves 4 to 6

Garlic Marinated Broccoli

A fine dish that shows off the flavor of fresh-picked broccoli. Great for icebox raids.

1 large head broccoli, cut into
small 2- to 3-inch florets

MARINADE:
3 tablespoons olive oil
1 teaspoon finely minced garlic
2 tablespoons chopped fresh
basil or 1 tablespoon dried
1 teaspoon chopped fresh
oregano or ½ teaspoon dried
2 teaspoons soy sauce
2 tablespoons vinegar
freshly ground pepper to taste

Mix the marinade ingredients together. Steam or quickly boil broccoli florets only until they are tender-crisp. Drain immediately and chill broccoli in ice water to set color and stop the cooking process. Toss the well-drained broccoli with the marinade and let flavors blend for at least ½ hour. Serve at room temperature or chilled.

Serves 4

Broccoli with Buttered Crumbs

These golden crumbs with their hint of pungent rosemary combine perfectly with the robust flavor of fresh broccoli. Another example of simply combining delicious flavors for a fine dish.

2 tablespoons butter
1 cup fresh bread crumbs
¼ cup chopped fresh parsley, packed firmly
1 teaspoon minced fresh rosemary or ½ teaspoon dried
salt and pepper to taste
1½ pounds broccoli, cut into florets
2 teaspoons melted butter
1 tablespoon lemon juice

Melt butter in a heavy skillet over low heat. Add the bread crumbs and cook, stirring constantly, until they are golden brown. Transfer to a bowl. Blend parsley and rosemary together then combine with the crumbs. Season with salt and pepper. Separately steam the broccoli just until tender-crisp. Remove to a warm serving dish and stir in the melted butter and lemon juice. Salt and pepper to taste. Top with the breadcrumb mixture and serve.

Serves 4 to 6

Bright Broccoli Sauté

Eye-catching colors and crisp textures make this a tasty and healthy winner at the table.

1 tablespoon olive oil
2 large cloves garlic, finely diced
1 large onion, halved and very thinly sliced
2 red bell peppers, seeded and thinly sliced
3 cups broccoli florets, cut into bite-sized pieces
3 tablespoons pine nuts or almonds, lightly toasted if you have time
salt and pepper to taste

Heat oil in a large, deep skillet. Sauté garlic and onions until soft and translucent. Add peppers and stir-fry for several minutes. Add broccoli and nuts and stir-fry until broccoli is just tender-crisp. Season with salt and pepper to taste and serve right away.

Serves 6

LEMONY BAKED BROCCOLI

An appetizing and brightly colored dish that showcases fine fresh broccoli.

> 2 medium heads broccoli,
>   cut into medium florets
>   with 1-inch stems (about
>   1¼ to 1½ pounds total)
> 1 teaspoon grated lemon rind
> 2 tablespoons lemon juice
> 2 tablespoons finely chopped
>   fresh parsley
> ¼ cup finely chopped fresh basil
> freshly ground pepper to taste
> ⅓ cup fresh or canned tomato
>   sauce
> 4 ounces mozzarella cheese,
>   thinly sliced, or 1 cup grated

Preheat oven to 350°F.

Bring a pot of water to a boil and boil or steam the broccoli until it is tender-crisp but not overcooked! Immediately transfer to a bowl of ice water to stop the cooking process and to keep the broccoli bright green. Drain. Put the broccoli into a well-buttered casserole dish and sprinkle with lemon rind, lemon juice, parsley and basil. Add pepper to taste. Spread the tomato sauce over top and cover with the cheese. Bake until hot and bubbly—about 10 minutes. Serve immediately.

Serves 6

BROCCOLI WITH PINE NUTS

This recipe shows that less is more—its simplicity yields a delightful dish best made with the freshest broccoli, just harvested from the garden.

> 2 pounds very fresh broccoli
> 1 tablespoon olive oil
> 2 tablespoons unsalted butter
> 3 tablespoons freshly squeezed
>   lemon juice
> ⅓ to ½ cup pine nuts, lightly
>   toasted

Divide broccoli into florets about 3 inches long. (Save stems for another dish.) Drop broccoli florets into boiling salted water for a very brief time, no more than 2 minutes, cooking them just until tender-crisp. Drain immediately and put in ice water to stop cooking action. Drain and let dry on a clean kitchen towel or paper towel.

Heat oil in a skillet, add butter and melt. Whisk in lemon juice. Add the broccoli florets, stir to combine, and sauté for 3 to 5 minutes, turning the broccoli and stirring constantly. Add toasted pine nuts in the last few minutes of cooking and toss with broccoli, combining well to heat the nuts through. Serve immediately.

Serves 4

Brussels Sprouts

Brussels Sprouts and Carrots with Creamy Lemon-Poppyseed Dressing

A colorful and delicious fall dish.

> 5 tablespoons light olive oil
> 3 tablespoons fresh lemon juice
> 1½ teaspoons poppyseeds
> 1 teaspoon minced garlic
> ½ teaspoon Dijon mustard
> ¼ teaspoon salt
> pinch of cayenne pepper
> 1 egg
> 8 carrots, cut into ½-inch slices
> 1 pound brussels sprouts, trimmed
> 1 tablespoon chopped scallions

Whisk oil, lemon juice, poppyseeds, garlic, mustard, salt and cayenne pepper together until well blended. Heat a saucepan of water to boiling. Add the egg in shell; cook for one minute only. Break the egg into the sauce and whisk to blend. Steam the vegetables until tender-crisp, drain; pour sauce over vegetables and toss with vegetables to blend. Sprinkle the scallions over the top and serve. Serve hot or at room temperature.

Serves 4 to 6

Marinated Brussels Sprouts

A piquant and tasty way to eat your sprouts.

> 1 pound brussels sprouts
> 2 tablespoons sweet pickle relish
> 2 tablespoons chopped pimiento or red bell pepper
> 2 tablespoons finely chopped scallions
> ¼ cup dry white wine
> 1 tablespoon vinegar
> 1 teaspoon Dijon mustard
> 2 tablespoons vegetable oil
> 1 clove garlic, minced
> ½ teaspoon salt
> ¼ teaspoon pepper

Trim and clean brussels sprouts. Steam or boil them in a small amount of water until tender but firm. Drain and cool quickly in ice water to stop the cooking process. In a medium bowl, combine the rest of the ingredients and mix together. Add the drained brussels sprouts and toss lightly. Cover and refrigerate for at least an hour to let the flavors blend. Serve chilled or at room temperature.

Serves 4 to 6

BRUSSELS SPROUTS AND CORN CRUSTLESS QUICHE

This recipe brings out the natural sweet nuttiness of both vegetables.

12 brussels sprouts, trimmed
   and halved
1 tablespoon butter
1½ cups whole milk
2 large eggs
2 tablespoons all-purpose flour
1 teaspoon salt
1½ teaspoons sugar
½ teaspoon finely chopped fresh
   oregano or ¼ teaspoon dried
2 tablespoons finely chopped
   parsley
¼ teaspoon ground nutmeg
2 cups cooked, drained corn
   (frozen corn, thawed, okay)
4 to 5 scallions, thinly sliced

Preheat oven to 350°F.

Blanch brussels sprouts for one minute in boiling water. Drain and run immediately under cold water to stop cooking. Drain again and place cut-side-down in an 8- or 9-inch casserole dish. Melt the butter in a saucepan, add milk and heat through until warm. In a bowl, beat eggs lightly, then add flour, salt, sugar, herbs and nutmeg. Mix in combined milk and butter, then add corn and scallions. Pour over brussels sprouts. Bake casserole 40 to 45 minutes and serve hot or at room temperature.

Serves 6

CABBAGE

BAKED CABBAGE CASSEROLE DINNER

Satisfying and full-flavored dish but not at all rich.
Makes a whole dinner if combined with crusty bread and a good jug of burgundy.

2 tablespoons butter or oil
2 large onions, thinly sliced
12 ounces mild Italian sausage
3 large, tart apples, cored and
  thinly sliced
3 tablespoons all-purpose flour
1 small head cabbage (about 1½
  pounds), coarsely shredded
¼ teaspoon salt
freshly ground pepper
¼ teaspoon ground nutmeg
½ cup chicken stock
2 teaspoons lemon juice

TOPPING:
Combine well:
¾ cup bread crumbs
¾ cup coarsely grated sharp
  Cheddar cheese
1 tablespoon minced parsley

Preheat oven to 375°F.

Melt butter and sauté onions until softened. Remove from pan and reserve. Remove casing from sausage and sauté until cooked through, breaking up the meat. Drain and reserve. Combine apples with flour. Lightly grease a deep 2½-quart casserole dish. Cover bottom with half the cabbage, then a layer of half of the apples, half the sausage and half the onions. Sprinkle with half of the salt, pepper to taste and half of the nutmeg. Repeat with another layer of cabbage, apples, sausage, onions and seasonings. Combine chicken stock and lemon juice and spoon over top. Cover tightly with foil (and casserole lid if available) and bake for 45 to 50 minutes or until tender. Remove foil, sprinkle with crumb topping and bake uncovered for 15 minutes more or until golden and crunchy. Serve hot.

Serves 6

California Cabbage Salad Supper

A complete meal when served with hot, crusty French bread and a good full-bodied red wine.

> 4 thick slices bacon
> 2 to 3 scallions, finely chopped
> 1 small head green or red cabbage, cored and shredded
> 3 tablespoons good red wine vinegar
> 1 four-ounce package of garlic and herb Alouette cheese or similar herb-flavored cream cheese
> freshly ground black pepper
> chopped fresh parsley

In a 12-inch skillet, fry the bacon until crisp. Remove from pan and crumble it into fairly large bits. Pour out all but 2 tablespoons of the bacon drippings. Add the scallions to the drippings and fry until limp and transparent.

Add the shredded cabbage and cook over high heat, stirring constantly until the cabbage begins to wilt. Add the crumbled bacon and the wine vinegar.

Divide the cabbage between two large dinner plates. Cut the Alouette cheese in half and top each plate of cabbage with one half of the cheese placed in the center of the hot cabbage portions.

Grind black pepper over all, and sprinkle with fresh parsley. Serve immediately, while still nicely hot. The cheese will begin to melt into the hot sautéed cabbage and each diner can enjoy the combination of flavors.

Serves 2

Alsatian Dilled Cabbage

A hearty, filling dish for a cold fall evening. Excellent with pork, chicken, sausages or frankfurters.

> 4 tablespoons butter
> ½ cup chopped onions
> 1 small, firm head cabbage (about 2½ pounds), cut into ½-inch dice
> ½ teaspoon salt
> 4 teaspoons chopped fresh dill or 1 tablespoon dried
> 1 tablespoon all-purpose flour
> 1 cup sour cream (don't substitute)
> 1 tablespoon mild vinegar
> 1 teaspoon sugar

Melt the butter in a large, deep pan and sauté the chopped onions until softened and slightly golden in color. Add the diced cabbage, salt and dill, and stir to mix together. Cover the pan and cook over medium heat until the cabbage is just tender-crisp—don't overcook. Remove from heat briefly while you stir the flour into the sour cream. Put the cabbage back over medium heat, add the sour cream mixture and cook, stirring, until the cabbage is glazed and thickened, about 3 to 5 minutes. Add the vinegar and sugar. Stir to blend and serve immediately.

Serves 6

LEMON BUTTERED CABBAGE

¼ cup butter
½ teaspoon caraway or celery seed
1 medium head cabbage, coarsely
  chopped
peel and juice of ½ lemon
freshly ground pepper to taste

Melt the butter with the seed in a
large frying pan. Add the cabbage
and cook, stirring constantly, over
high heat, 3 to 4 minutes. Reduce the
heat and cover. Simmer 3 minutes
only until just tender. Chop lemon
peel coarsely and add along with
juice and pepper. Serve right away.

Serves 4

SWEET AND SOUR SAUTÉED CABBAGE

½ each small to medium heads
  red and green cabbage (or all
  of one color)
¼ cup butter
1 large or 2 small red apples,
  chopped into ½-inch dice
3 tablespoons fresh lemon juice
2½ tablespoons firmly packed
  brown sugar
2 tablespoons cider vinegar
½ teaspoon salt
¼ teaspoon freshly ground
  pepper
¼ teaspoon ground cloves

Coarsely shred cabbage and set aside.
Melt butter in a heavy skillet. Add
apple and cook, stirring, for about
3 to 5 minutes, until it begins to
soften. Mix in the lemon juice, brown
sugar, vinegar, salt, pepper and
cloves. Add cabbage and stir-fry
until the cabbage is tender but still
crunchy—about 5 to 6 minutes. Serve
right away.

Serves 4

PICKLED PAK CHOI

*A colorful snack—not too tart or too
sweet, but crunchy and tasty. Keeps well
in the refrigerator for extended enjoyment.*

2 cups water
1 cup red wine vinegar
½ cup sugar
⅔ cup dry sherry
1 teaspoon salt
4 large stalks pak choi (bok choi)
  or 6 to 8 small stalks, cut into
  ½-inch diagonal pieces
3 carrots, peeled and cut into
  ½-inch diagonal slices
3 scallions, cut into 1-inch pieces
1 teaspoon mustard seed
1 tablespoon finely chopped
  fresh ginger
2 small dried red chile peppers,
  seeds removed and coarsely
  chopped
optional: 1 clove garlic, halved

In a medium saucepan, combine
water, vinegar, sugar, sherry and
salt. Heat, stirring until sugar
is dissolved. Simmer 5 minutes, then
cool to room temperature.

Place the vegetables in a 1-quart
jar. Stir mustard seed, ginger, red
peppers and garlic into cooled vinegar
mixture and pour over vegetables.
Cover jar tightly and refrigerate at
least 2 days before serving.

Makes 1 quart

CARROTS

CARROT BRAN MUFFINS

Fine and rich tasting with the extra nutrition and goodness of sweet carrots.

1½ cups all-purpose flour
1½ teaspoons baking powder
½ teaspoon baking soda
1 teaspoon cinnamon
¼ teaspoon nutmeg
¼ teaspoon salt
1¼ cups bran
½ cup currants
2 eggs
⅔ cup firmly packed dark
  brown sugar
½ cup vegetable oil
1½ cups finely grated carrots
1 cup buttermilk
1 teaspoon vanilla
6 dates, cut in half

Preheat oven to 350°F.

On a sheet of waxed paper or in a bowl, sift together the flour, baking powder, baking soda, cinnamon, nutmeg and salt. Stir in bran and currants. Set aside. In a large bowl, beat eggs lightly, add brown sugar, vegetable oil, carrots, buttermilk and vanilla, mixing until well blended. Add the dry ingredients into the egg mixture, mixing just until combined. Do not overmix. Spoon into greased muffin tins, filling them two-thirds full; top each with a date half. Bake 25 to 30 minutes until muffins pull away from sides of the pan.

Makes 12 to 14 muffins

PICKLED BABY CARROTS

Especially nice made with our round baby carrots.

1 pound freshly picked baby
  carrots
2 cups water
½ cup white wine vinegar
1 teaspoon each salt, mustard
  seed and peppercorns
1 bay leaf
1 tablespoon sugar

Trim carrots at both ends and scrub well. Combine carrots with remaining ingredients and cook 6 to 8 minutes until tender but still crisp. (Cooking time will depend on the size of carrots.) Cool the carrots in the liquid, then chill in covered glass jar(s) in the refrigerator. They will keep nicely for a week to 10 days in the refrigerator (if you don't eat them all first).

Makes approximately 2 cups

Carrots with Lemon and Dill

Dill and carrots not only look well together but taste terrific when paired up.

> **1 pound carrots, cut into ½-inch slices**
> **2 tablespoons butter**
> **½ cup minced onion**
> **¼ cup dry white wine**
> **½ teaspoon grated lemon zest (yellow part of peel)**
> **1 to 2 tablespoons lemon juice**
> **2 tablespoons minced fresh dill**
> **salt and white pepper to taste**

Steam carrots for about 7 minutes until tender-crisp. In a skillet, heat butter until foamy; add onion and sauté until softened. Add carrots, wine, lemon rind and one tablespoon of the lemon juice, and cook, stirring until most of the liquid is reduced, about 2 minutes. Add the dill, salt and white pepper and additional lemon juice to taste. Serve hot.

Serves 4

Carrots with Lime Butter Sauce

A tropical touch of lime enhances tender-crisp carrots.

> **2 tablespoons butter**
> **2 scallions, chopped**
> **1 pound carrots, cut in ½-inch chunks**
> **zest of 1 lime (green part of peel)**
> **2 tablespoons fresh lime juice**
> **salt and pepper to taste**
> **2 tablespoons chopped parsley**
>
> **OPTIONAL GARNISH:**
> **2 tablespoons very finely chopped nuts**

Melt butter in a large skillet. Add scallions and carrots and sauté together 2 to 3 minutes. Add lime zest and juice, cover and cook over low heat until carrots are just tender-crisp. Add salt and pepper to taste. Garnish with chopped parsley, adding nuts if desired.

Serves 4 to 6

Cinnamon Glazed Carrots

2 tablespoons butter
1½ pounds carrots, trimmed,
  scrubbed and left whole if
  young, quartered if mature
½ teaspoon salt
2 teaspoons sugar
water
½ teaspoon ground cinnamon

In a saucepan, melt the butter. Then add carrots, salt and sugar and enough water to barely cover the carrots. Cover and cook just until the carrots are tender. (Time will vary depending on age and size of carrots.) Remove the lid. Bring to a boil and cook until the water has completely evaporated, leaving the carrots coated with a sticky, buttery glaze. Sprinkle with the cinnamon, mix and serve immediately.

Serves 4 to 6

Fresh Carrots with Apricots

2 tablespoons butter
2 tablespoons water
1 pound fresh carrots, shredded
6 dried apricots, finely sliced
1 tablespoon sugar
1 tablespoon good white wine
  vinegar

Heat butter and water in a large skillet over medium-high heat. Add carrots and apricots. Sauté 2 to 3 minutes. Sprinkle the sugar over the top. Add vinegar. Stir and cook rapidly for 1 minute until nicely glazed. Serve immediately.

Serves 4

French Braised Carrots and Turnips

The sweet flavors and succulent textures of this dish will be enjoyed by carrot lovers who usually "hate turnips."

1 pound carrots, peeled and
  sliced ½ inch thick (baby
  carrots are delicious in this)
1 pound turnips, peeled, halved
  and sliced slightly thicker than
  the carrots
2 cups chicken stock
2 teaspoons sugar
2 tablespoons butter
salt and pepper to taste

GARNISH:
chopped fresh chives

Place the carrots and turnips in a large, heavy saucepan with the chicken stock, sugar, butter and salt and pepper to taste. Cook them, partially covered, over medium heat until they are tender, about 20 minutes (less if vegetables are quite fresh). Check the seasoning. Sprinkle with chopped chives and serve in a warmed serving dish.

Serves 4 to 6

Baby Carrots and Beets with Tarragon Yogurt Dip

1 pound each baby carrots and beets, poached or steamed, cooled and arranged on a platter

DIP:
1½ cups yogurt
½ cup mayonnaise
2 large cloves garlic, minced
2 tablespoons chopped fresh tarragon leaves or 1 tablespoon dried
¼ teaspoon salt
2 tablespoons red wine vinegar
1 tablespoon sugar or honey

Blend together the dip ingredients and taste for seasoning. Allow dip to stand for ½ hour to blend flavors and serve with baby carrots and beets as a first course or appetizer. Leftover dip can also be used as a salad dressing.

Serves 6 as an appetizer

Carrot Salad del Sol

The tang of ginger melds perfectly with carrots, lemon and raisins.

4 cups shredded carrots
2 tablespoons lemon juice
pinch salt
⅓ cup finely chopped candied grapefruit or orange rind
¼ cup finely chopped candied ginger
¾ cup chopped golden raisins or currants
optional: raw cashews or sunflower seeds

Combine all the ingredients and let the flavors blend for a few hours.

Serves 4 to 6

Baby Carrots with Ginger and Sage Butter

2 pounds baby carrots, scrubbed
½ cup unsalted butter
1½ tablespoons brown sugar
2 tablespoons chopped fresh ginger
juice of ½ lemon
¼ teaspoon salt
1 large clove garlic, minced
1 tablespoon chopped fresh sage or 2 teaspoons dried

Poach carrots in water or chicken stock until just tender. Melt butter and add all other ingredients, then add the drained carrots and sauté 2 to 3 minutes to blend flavors.

Serves 6

GOLDEN CARROT PIE

The carrots give this delectable pie a beautiful deep persimmon color that makes it even more appetizing.

2 pounds carrots, thinly sliced
2 tablespoons butter
⅓ cup brown sugar, firmly packed
2 teaspoons grated orange zest (orange part of peel)
1 tablespoon all-purpose flour
½ teaspoon cinnamon
½ teaspoon ground ginger
¼ teaspoon nutmeg
pinch salt
2 eggs
1 cup evaporated milk
1 teaspoon vanilla
1 unbaked 9-inch pie shell

Preheat oven to 425°F.

Steam carrots until very tender. Purée in a food processor or blender. Then add butter, brown sugar and orange rind. Add to this mixture the flour, cinnamon, ginger, nutmeg and salt. Blend well. When mixture has cooled, beat in eggs, evaporated milk and vanilla, mixing only until combined. Do not overblend. Pour into pie shell. Bake in the lower third of the oven 20 minutes, then reduce heat to 350°F and bake 45 minutes longer or until a knife inserted near the edge comes out clean. Cool on rack.

Serves 6 to 8

CHOCOLATE CHIP CARROT CAKE

An irresistible cake; be prepared to share this recipe!

1 cup unsalted butter, at room temperature
2 cups sugar
3 eggs
2½ cups all-purpose flour
1 teaspoon baking soda
1 teaspoon cinnamon
½ teaspoon nutmeg
½ teaspoon allspice
2 tablespoons baking cocoa
½ cup water
1 tablespoon vanilla
2 cups shredded carrots
¾ cup chopped nuts
¾ cup chocolate chips

Preheat oven to 350°F.

Cream butter and sugar until light and fluffy. Add eggs one at a time, beating well after each addition. Sift dry ingredients together; add to creamed mixture alternately with water and vanilla. Fold in carrots, nuts and chips. Turn into a greased and floured 9 × 13-inch pan. Bake for 45 minutes. Cool and top with our Cream Cheese Frosting.

CREAM CHEESE FROSTING:
¼ cup butter, at room temperature
6 to 8 ounces cream cheese, at room temperature
½ teaspoon vanilla
1 teaspoon grated orange zest (orange part of peel)
2 cups powdered sugar, measured and then sifted
2 to 3 tablespoons milk

Cream butter, cheese, vanilla, orange peel. Gradually mix in powdered sugar. Add milk gradually, thinning frosting to desired consistency.

Serves 16 to 18

CAULIFLOWER

CRUMBLE-TOPPED CAULIFLOWER

The smoothness of the cauliflower matches up well with this tasty crumble topping.

 1 head cauliflower, broken
  into florets
 2 tablespoons olive oil
 2 tablespoons butter
 2 hard-boiled eggs, finely
  chopped
 ¾ teaspoon ground cumin
 ⅓ cup bread crumbs
 ¼ cup grated Parmesan cheese
 salt and pepper to taste
 3 tablespoons finely chopped
  parsley

Drop cauliflower florets into a saucepan of boiling water and cook just until tender—3 to 5 minutes. Drain. Melt the oil and butter in a skillet, add cauliflower and stir briefly, just until pieces begin to color. Mix together all other ingredients and spread over top of cauliflower. Heat through so cheese melts, then serve right away.

Serves 4

YOGURT CURRIED CAULIFLOWER

The creamy cauliflower combines perfectly with the smooth yogurt and curry sauce.

 1 large head cauliflower
 1 tablespoon butter
 1 cup fresh plain yogurt
 ½ teaspoon good curry powder
 2 teaspoons seasoned bread
  crumbs

Steam the cauliflower whole, just until tender. Do not overcook! Remove the cauliflower carefully to serving plate and dot with butter. Combine the yogurt and curry powder and spread over the cauliflower. Sprinkle with bread crumbs and serve promptly.

Serves 4 to 6

CHEESY CAULIFLOWER BAKE

Just as warm and comforting as rich mashed potatoes but without the heaviness. Garden fresh, sweet cauliflower makes all the difference in this recipe.

1 medium to large head
   cauliflower, cut into florets
2 tablespoons butter
2 tablespoons milk or cream
½ teaspoon salt
freshly ground white pepper
   to taste
½ cup grated Swiss cheese
¼ teaspoon grated nutmeg
3 tablespoons each bread crumbs
   and freshly grated Parmesan
   cheese

Cook cauliflower until very tender by steaming or cooking in boiling water. Drain. Thoroughly mash using a potato masher or food processor and add the butter, milk, salt, pepper and grated Swiss cheese, combining well. Put the cauliflower mixture into a well-buttered casserole dish and sprinkle with the nutmeg, bread crumbs and Parmesan. Bake until hot and bubbly—about 10 to 15 minutes at 350°F. Serve immediately.

Serves 4

WYN'S BROILED CAULIFLOWER

When our cauliflowers were cut in the trial garden this summer, everyone wanted to make a whole meal of this one dish.

Preheat the broiler.
   Break a head of cauliflower into florets and steam briefly until just tender—don't overcook. Arrange the florets on a broiler pan and brush them with melted or softened butter, then a layer of grated Parmesan cheese and a very generous dusting of paprika. Broil until cheese bubbles and begins to brown. Serve right away.

Serves 4

CHARD

MILANESE-STYLE CHARD

A fine northern Italian dish that marries chard's full flavor with a delicious herb-based sauce.

1 bunch (1 pound) Swiss chard
2 tablespoons olive oil
1 clove garlic, minced
6 scallions, thinly sliced
2 tablespoons chopped fresh
**   parsley**
¼ cup chopped fresh basil
pinch nutmeg
¼ cup chopped prosciutto
**   or ham**
2 tablespoons freshly grated
**   Parmesan cheese**
salt and freshly ground pepper
**   to taste**

GARNISH:
2 tablespoons toasted pine
**   nuts or chopped walnuts**

Trim the chard, discarding tough stems, and coarsely chop.

In a large, deep skillet, heat olive oil, add garlic and scallions and sauté until softened and fragrant, 2 to 3 minutes. Add chard, parsley, basil, nutmeg, prosciutto or ham and mix together well. Cover the skillet and cook over medium heat until tender and wilted, 3 to 5 minutes. Mix in Parmesan cheese and then add salt and pepper to taste. Serve garnished with the pine nuts or walnuts.

Serves 4 to 6

Juicy Sautéed Swiss Chard

A wonderfully easy way to make chard into one of your family's most favored vegetables.

1 bunch (1 pound) Swiss chard
2 tablespoons olive oil
1 clove garlic, minced
6 scallions, thinly sliced
2 medium tomatoes, peeled,
  diced and drained
2 tablespoons red wine vinegar
2 teaspoons sugar
⅛ teaspoon Tabasco sauce
¼ cup chopped fresh basil
¼ cup sour cream (lowfat okay)
salt and freshly ground pepper
  to taste

Trim the chard, discarding any tough stems. In a large skillet, heat olive oil, add garlic and scallions and sauté until softened, 2 to 3 minutes. Add chard, tossing to coat leaves. Cover pan with a lid and heat for 3 to 5 minutes until chard is wilted and tender. Add tomatoes, vinegar, sugar, Tabasco sauce and basil. Heat through for 2 to 3 minutes. Remove from stove and mix in sour cream. Add salt and pepper to taste and serve.

Serves 4 to 6

Chard with Beet Vinegar

The colorful, vibrant sweet-and-sour sauce combines with the smooth finish of sour cream to really set off the flavor of the chard.

2 large beets, peeled and cooked
1 cup rice vinegar
3 tablespoons sugar
½ teaspoon lemon juice
dash white pepper
1 large bunch fresh chard or
  beet greens, chopped
butter to taste

GARNISH:
sour cream or fresh plain yogurt

In a blender, purée the beets together with the rice vinegar, sugar, lemon juice and white pepper. Pour into a non-aluminum saucepan and bring to a boil. Reduce heat and simmer, covered, 5 minutes. Cool. Steam the chard until tender, drain. Toss chard with butter and pepper to taste. Arrange the cooked chard on a serving platter. Spoon over some of the beet vinegar to taste and garnish with a very generous dollop of sour cream or yogurt.

Serves 4

California Stuffed Chard

Bright green chard leaves make perfect wrappers for this handsome entrée, which is halfway between stuffed grape leaves and stuffed cabbage but lighter than either dish. One of my all-time favorite recipes.

MEAT FILLING:
1¼ pounds ground veal or turkey
¼ pound lean ground pork
1 large clove garlic, chopped
¼ teaspoon nutmeg
½ teaspoon pepper
1 teaspoon salt
¼ cup parsley
1 teaspoon each chopped fresh
   oregano and thyme or
   ½ teaspoon each dried
½ teaspoon Tabasco sauce
2 teaspoons Worcestershire sauce
1 egg, beaten
¼ cup milk

15 chard leaves, stems removed
   and reserved
2 tablespoons butter
2 medium onions, chopped
2 cups chicken stock
2 tablespoons lemon juice
1 to 2 tablespoons good, fruity
   olive oil

GARNISH:
lemon slices
fresh yogurt or sour cream

Mix the meat filling ingredients together until well combined and set aside.

Immerse the chard leaves, 4 or 5 at a time, in a pot of boiling water for 2 minutes or until limp. Remove with a slotted spoon and drain well. Repeat with all the leaves and drain. Discard the water.

Lay chard leaves out flat. Mound several rounded tablespoons of the reserved meat filling on the center of each leaf. Fold sides of leaf over center, then fold top and bottom down. Roll each leaf into a compact bundle. (Can be made ahead until this point.)

Finely chop reserved chard stems. In a large heavy pot, melt 2 tablespoons butter over medium heat. Sauté the chopped onions and chard stems for 5 minutes or until the onion is soft. Lay chard bundles on top of the sautéed vegetables, add chicken stock and sprinkle with lemon juice. Bring to a boil, then reduce heat to a simmer. Drizzle 1 to 2 tablespoons olive oil over the bundles. Simmer over low heat until filling is done—about 35 minutes. Garnish savory chard bundles with fresh lemon slices and pass fresh yogurt or sour cream to top the bundles.

Serves 6 to 8

Bountiful Lasagne

A real crowd pleaser, this dish will serve 16 people in a very satisfying manner, or the recipe can be halved to serve 6 to 8. Leftovers are delicious reheated in the microwave.

> 20 lasagne noodles
> 3 large bunches fresh chard
>   or spinach
> ⅔ cup chopped onion
> 2 cloves garlic, minced
> 2 tablespoons olive oil
> 2 cups grated raw carrots
> 3 cups sliced fresh mushrooms
> 2 fifteen-ounce cans tomato sauce
>   (or use thick homemade)
> 1 cup chopped pitted olives
> 4 teaspoons chopped fresh
>   oregano or 2 teaspoons dried
> 3 cups ricotta or cream-style
>   cottage cheese
> ¾ pound Monterey jack or
>   mozzarella cheese, thinly sliced
> ¾ cup grated Parmesan cheese

Cook noodles in boiling salted water for 8 to 10 minutes. Drain. Wash chard or spinach well and cook very briefly in a small amount of boiling water—about 3 to 6 minutes. Drain very well and chop. In a large skillet, sauté the onion and garlic in the oil until soft. Add the carrots, mushrooms, tomato sauce, olives and oregano and heat thoroughly.

Preheat oven to 375°F. Oil a large, deep casserole or pan. Layer one-half each of the noodles, ricotta or cottage cheese, drained chopped chard or spinach, sauce mixture and cheese slices. Repeat, placing remaining one-half of the Monterey jack slices on top. Sprinkle with the grated Parmesan cheese. Bake for 30 to 45 minutes, until hot and bubbly.

Serves 14 to 16

Brodo de Bietola e Risotto
Chicken, Chard and Rice Soup

This is a warm, rich-flavored soup that can be a whole meal in itself with hot, crusty bread and butter.

> 2 bunches (about 1½ pounds)
>   freshly picked chard
> ¼ cup butter
> ¼ cup chopped onion
> 6 to 7 cups chicken stock
> ¾ cup Italian or short-grained
>   white rice
> ½ cup freshly grated Parmesan
>   cheese
> 1 tablespoon minced parsley
> salt to taste
>
> GARNISH:
> additional Parmesan cheese

Wash the chard well and cut both leaves and stalks into ½-inch-wide strips. In a 4- or 5-quart pot, melt the butter. Add the onion and sauté over medium heat until softened. Add the chard and stir to coat with butter. Cover the pot and heat for 4 to 5 minutes to wilt the chard.

Add 6 cups chicken stock; bring to a boil and add the rice. Cover and cook over medium heat until the rice is done, about 20 minutes. If the soup becomes too thick, add more stock. When the rice is done, add the fresh Parmesan and the parsley. Taste for seasoning. Serve piping hot sprinkled with more cheese.

Serves 6 to 8

CHILE PEPPERS

*N*ot all chile peppers are hot and there is much more to their flavor than most
of us realize—until we try them! While there probably isn't a country in the world
that doesn't grow some kind of pepper as a condiment, spice or vegetable, many of us
are just discovering the diversity of their flavors and shapes. Each chile type has a
distinctive taste, from mild and rich to spicy and piquant to fiery hot. Roasting imparts
yet another, earthier flavor. To roast chiles, put them on a baking sheet and place
under preheated broiler about 4 inches from heat. Turn them until blistered and
charred, about 10 to 12 minutes. Enclose the peppers in a paper bag and let
them steam until they are cool enough to handle. Starting at the blossom end,
peel the peppers under cold water, discarding the stems, ribs and seeds.

CHILE-CHEESE PAN SOUFFLÉ

*A light and satisfying one-dish meal. Try
it with a simple salad and warm, crusty
bread.*

    ¼ cup butter, melted and cooled
    5 eggs
    ¼ cup all-purpose flour
    ½ teaspoon baking powder
    ¼ teaspoon salt
    ½ cup peeled and roasted
      chopped poblano chiles
    1 cup cottage cheese (small curd)
    8 ounces Monterey jack cheese
      (or half Cheddar, half jack)

Preheat oven to 350°F.
   Melt the butter in an 8-inch-square
pan. In a bowl lightly beat the eggs.
Add the flour, baking powder and
salt and blend until mixed. Add the
melted butter from the baking pan,
the chiles, cottage and Monterey jack
cheeses. Mix until just blended. Pour
into the pan in which the butter was
melted. Bake for 35 minutes or until
puffed and golden brown. Serve
immediately.

Serves 6 to 8

CHILE-OLIVE DIP

    2 cans sliced black olives
    8 to 10 poblano chiles, roasted,
      peeled and chopped, about 1 cup
    3 scallions, cut into 1-inch lengths
    1 small tomato, quartered and
      drained
    2 tablespoons vegetable oil
    2 tablespoons cider vinegar
    1 tablespoon chopped fresh
      cilantro leaves

Combine all ingredients in a blender
and process until barely blended.
Serve as a dip with sliced jicama
and/or tortilla chips.

Makes about 2 cups

HOT PEPPER JELLY

Delicious with cream cheese or on dark breads. Also good with cold-cut sandwiches or with baked ham.

> 5 medium jalapeño chiles
> 2 small green bell peppers and
>   1 small red bell pepper (or an
>   additional green one)
> 6 cups sugar
> 2 cups cider vinegar
> 1 six-ounce bottle or 2 three-
>   ounce pouches liquid pectin
> optional: several drops of red
>   or green food coloring

Wear rubber gloves and split open the jalapeños. Remove and discard seeds and coarsely chop chiles. Repeat with bell peppers. Place all the peppers in a blender or food processor and purée until liquefied. (Add a bit of the vinegar if needed to make blending easier.) You should have about 1 cup.

In a large (5-quart) pot combine the puréed peppers with the sugar and vinegar over high heat. Bring to a rolling boil, stirring constantly, add the pectin and return to a rolling boil. Boil for exactly one minute.

Remove from heat, add coloring if desired, skim and immediately pour into 6 half-pint canning jars. Complete the seals by processing in a boiling-water bath for 10 minutes or using paraffin wax.

Makes about 6 cups

MEXICAN FONDUE

This dish is easy to put together quickly for a special treat or unexpected company, and everyone will enjoy it.

> 1 fifteen-ounce can refried beans
> ½ pound Cheddar cheese, grated
> 2 tablespoons butter
> 2 tablespoons minced scallion
> 1 clove garlic, minced
> ½ teaspoon Worcestershire sauce
> 1 cayenne pepper, seeded and
>   chopped
> 1 Anaheim or poblano chile,
>   seeded and chopped
> ¾ cup beer at room temperature

Combine all the ingredients except the beer in a heavy saucepan. Heat, stirring, until mixture is heated through, 10 to 15 minutes. Add beer gradually, stirring. Transfer to a fondue pot.

Accompany with tortilla chips or fresh vegetables for dipping.

Makes about 3 cups

Four-Alarm Cayenne Chicken

The chiles season this dish beautifully, but they are very hot. Warn diners not to eat them!

SEASONING SAUCE:
1 teaspoon cornstarch
½ teaspoon grated fresh ginger
 or ¼ teaspoon dried
1 tablespoon sherry
2 tablespoons soy sauce
1½ teaspoons sugar
2 teaspoons red wine vinegar
1 teaspoon chile paste with garlic
2 teaspoons hoisin sauce
3 tablespoons chicken stock
1 teaspoon sesame oil

1½ pounds skinned and boned
 chicken breast, cut into
 2-inch strips
1 tablespoon cornstarch
1 tablespoon soy sauce
1 egg white, slightly beaten
1 clove garlic, minced
cooking oil
12 dried cayenne chiles, halved
 and seeded

GARNISH:
½ cup dry roasted peanuts

Prepare seasoning sauce by mixing together ingredients. Set aside.

Place chicken in a small bowl with cornstarch, soy sauce, egg white and garlic. Mix well and refrigerate for ½ hour.

Heat 2 tablespoons of cooking oil in a wok or heavy skillet. Add chiles and cook until dark—about 15 seconds. Lower heat, add chicken and cook through—about 2 or 3 minutes. Add seasoning sauce and cook another minute until well combined and hot. Serve, sprinkling with the peanuts, over hot fluffy rice.

Serves 4

Tex-Mex Casserole

This savory vegetable casserole is also very good the next day and makes a great lunch "leftover" meal.

4 ears fresh corn
¼ cup butter
3 medium onions, thinly sliced
6 or 7 medium zucchinis,
 thinly sliced
1 large tomato, seeded,
 chopped and drained
1 eight-ounce can of tomatillos,
 drained and diced, or
1 cup fresh
2 Anaheim chiles, seeded
 and chopped
1 small jalapeño chile, seeded
 and chopped
1½ teaspoons chopped fresh
 oregano or ¾ teaspoon dried
salt and pepper to taste
1 cup grated Monterey jack or
 Cheddar cheese

Preheat oven to 350°F.

Using a very sharp knife, cut the corn from the cobs and set aside. In a large skillet, heat a tablespoon of the butter and sauté the onions and zucchini for 3 to 5 minutes over medium heat. Remove. Add another tablespoon or two of the butter and sauté the tomato and tomatillos for 3 to 5 minutes. Lightly grease a large casserole. Combine all the vegetables together, including chiles; season with oregano, salt and pepper. Sprinkle with the grated cheese and dot with the remaining tablespoon of butter.

Bake the casserole, covered with its lid or with foil, for 30 minutes. Then run it briefly under the broiler to brown the top before serving.

Serves 4 to 6

SALSA DE TOMATILLO

For a mild but piquant alternative to red tomato-based salsa, try this authentic and handsome green salsa. It's delicious with cold chicken, enchiladas, chips, etc.

> 2 pounds fresh tomatillos
> ½ cup water
> ½ teaspoon salt
> ¼ cup scallions, cut into 1-inch lengths
> ¼ cup fresh cilantro
> 3 or 4 fresh jalapeño chiles, trimmed, cored and seeded
> 1 teaspoon minced garlic
> ½ teaspoon sugar
> 1 teaspoon lemon juice

Peel husks off tomatillos; wash off sticky residue in cold water.

Bring water and salt to a boil in a medium saucepan. Add tomatillos and cook, covered, until softened, about 5 minutes. Remove from heat and transfer to a food processor or blender. Add remaining ingredients and process to a thick purée. Taste for seasoning.

Sauce can be stored tightly covered in refrigerator for up to 3 days.

Makes 3 to 4 cups

SALSA FRESCA

Perfect for dips or to spoon over barbecued chicken or hamburgers.

> 5 small tomatoes, finely chopped
> 8 scallions, white part only, coarsely chopped
> 1 large clove garlic, minced
> 1 or 2 fresh serrano or jalapeño chiles, seeded and finely chopped
> 3 or 4 mild green chiles, roasted, peeled, seeded and finely chopped
> 2 tablespoons chopped fresh cilantro
> ½ teaspoon salt
> pinch freshly ground pepper
> 1 teaspoon red wine vinegar

Combine all ingredients in a small bowl.

Note: Salsa is always best served fresh but may be kept for up to 2 days in refrigerator. It may get watery after storage; pour off any excess liquid before serving.

Makes 2½ cups

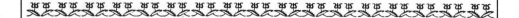

CHILE PEAR RELISH

2½ pounds fresh pears, peeled,
  cored and finely sliced
1 cup brown sugar, firmly packed
¾ cup cider vinegar
5 tablespoons water
3 tablespoons chopped onion
1 teaspoon salt
1 teaspoon chile powder
¼ teaspoon cumin
2 tablespoons chopped pimiento
4 tablespoons chopped green
  Anaheim chiles
1 serrano or jalapeño chile, seeded
  and finely chopped

Place all ingredients in a heavy
4- or 5-quart saucepan; stir to blend.
Cover and cook the mixture over low
heat for 30 minutes. If liquid has
evaporated, add an additional ¼ cup
water. Uncover and continue cooking for about 25 minutes or just until
the mixture has thickened, stirring
frequently. Serve cold. Keeps well in
the refrigerator.

Makes approximately 4 cups

CORRALITOS RICE CASSEROLE

A local favorite influenced by our ongoing love affair with Tex-Mex cuisine. Great for potlucks and big gatherings and generally loved by everyone!

> 3 cups cooked rice
> 2 cups "light" sour cream
> 5 scallions, chopped
> salt and pepper to taste
> 1½ cups cooked corn kernels
>   (about 2 ears)
> 3 Anaheim or poblano chiles,
>   roasted, peeled, seeded and
>   coarsely chopped (or use
>   2 four-ounce cans of
>   "California" mild green chiles)
> 1½ cups shredded Monterey
>   jack cheese
> ⅓ cup shredded Cheddar cheese

> GARNISH:
> 2 tablespoons chopped fresh
>   cilantro

Preheat oven to 350°F.

Mix the rice with the sour cream and scallions and add salt and pepper to taste. Spread half the rice mixture in the bottom of a greased 1½-quart casserole; top with half of the corn, half of the chiles, and half of the Monterey jack cheese. Repeat with the rest of the rice mixture, then the rest of the corn, chiles and jack cheese. Top with the Cheddar cheese.

Bake covered for 20 minutes, then uncover for 10 minutes to finish. Sprinkle with cilantro. Serve hot or warm.

Serves 6 to 8

CRAB-STUFFED CHILE RELLENOS

Low in calories; rich in flavor.

> 8 Anaheim chiles

> FILLING:
> ½ pound cooked crab meat
> 2 teaspoons fresh lemon juice
> 1 teaspoon hot mustard or
>   1½ teaspoons Dijon mustard
> 2 egg whites, lightly beaten
> 2 tablespoons finely chopped
>   fresh basil
> ¾ cup fresh bread crumbs

Preheat oven to 375°F.

Prepare chiles by roasting under broiler. Place in plastic bag to cool for 10 minutes. Peel the chiles under cold water. Slice open one side and remove seeds. Pat dry with paper towels.

Sprinkle crab with lemon juice. Stir in mustard, mixing well. Add egg whites and basil and blend. Add bread crumbs and toss mixture together. Open chiles flat and fill with filling, then fold chiles together. Place stuffed chiles on greased baking sheet, cover tightly with foil and bake for 20 minutes.

Serves 4 to 6

CHICKEN FAJITAS

*A juicy, mildly spicy light chicken dish that uses lots of fresh,
colorful sweet peppers. Quick and easy to make, we know it will bring
requests for second and even third helpings!*

3 Anaheim or poblano chiles,
  seeded and cut into strips or
  3 tablespoons chopped
  canned mild chiles
2 medium tomatoes, seeded
  and chopped
1 tablespoon finely chopped fresh
  oregano, or 2 teaspoons dried
1½ teaspoons ground cumin
1 tablespoon good quality
  chile powder
½ teaspoon salt
2 tablespoons all-purpose flour
1 pound skinned and boned chicken
  breasts, cut into ½-inch strips
4 tablespoons vegetable oil
1 large onion, thinly sliced
3 small cloves garlic, minced
3 large bell peppers, yellow, red
  and green (or at least 2 colors),
  thinly sliced
optional: 3 to 4 tablespoons chopped
  fresh cilantro
serve with warmed flour tortillas,
  sour cream and Salsa Fresca (p. 34)

Combine the chiles, tomatoes,
oregano, cumin, chile powder, salt
and flour with the chicken strips and
mix together well. Set aside to marinate briefly.

Heat 2 tablespoons of the oil in a
large, deep skillet and sauté the onion
and garlic until softened, 3 to 4 minutes. Add the bell pepper strips and
sauté about 5 minutes more, until the
peppers are slightly softened and
cooked, but still crisp. Remove from
skillet and keep warm.

Heat the remaining 2 tablespoons
of oil in the skillet. Sauté the marinated chicken strips, stirring and
tossing until strips are cooked
through and lose their pink color
when sliced. Add the sautéed pepper
mixture and heat and mix together
with chicken. Stir in cilantro if used.

Serve the fajitas mixture spooned
onto warm flour tortillas and pass
sour cream and salsa as condiments.
Each diner folds his or her tortilla
over the fajita mixture to enjoy.

Serves 4 to 6

Corn

Fresh Corn Muffins

Especially good served hot with honey.

- 1⅓ cups unbleached all-purpose flour
- 2½ teaspoons baking powder
- ½ teaspoon baking soda
- ½ teaspoon salt
- 3 tablespoons sugar
- ⅔ cup cornmeal
- 2 eggs, lightly beaten
- 1 cup buttermilk or fresh plain yogurt
- 2 tablespoons melted butter
- 1 cup cooked corn kernels (about 1 large ear)

Preheat oven to 375°F and lightly grease 12 muffin cups. Sift together the flour, baking powder, baking soda, salt and sugar. Mix in cornmeal. In a separate bowl, combine beaten eggs with the buttermilk or yogurt, melted butter and corn. Combine these wet ingredients with the dry ingredients, mixing just until blended; don't overmix. Spoon into muffin tins. Bake 20 to 25 minutes, until a cake tester inserted in center comes out clean.

Makes 12 muffins

Dried Corn Snack

For the corn-rich cook, this chewy and nutty-sweet natural snack is perfect for munching while watching fall games.

- 8 large ears fresh corn
- 3 tablespoons sugar
- 2 teaspoons salt
- ¼ cup milk

Preheat oven to 250°F.

Cut kernels from the cobs. Combine corn, sugar, salt and milk in a heavy-bottomed saucepan. Bring to a boil, then lower to simmer and cook for 15 minutes, stirring frequently. Pour into a shallow greased baking pan and dry in the oven for about 1½ hours, stirring occasionally. Corn should be light golden brown when done. Store in covered container for snacking.

Makes 7 to 8 cups

Fresh Tomato Corn Soup

The combined flavors of fresh sweet corn, tomatoes and herbs are unbeatable in this simple, light soup.

> 1 tablespoon butter
> 1 tablespoon olive oil
> 1½ cup chopped onions
> 2 pounds fresh tomatoes, peeled and coarsely chopped
> 1½ tablespoons tomato paste
> 4 cups chicken stock
> 1 teaspoon chopped fresh thyme or ½ teaspoon dried
> 1 teaspoon chopped fresh dill or ½ teaspoon dried
> ¼ cup packed fresh basil, chopped
> 2 cups fresh corn kernels
> salt and white pepper to taste

In a large saucepan, heat butter and olive oil, add onion and sauté until softened. Add tomatoes, tomato paste and chicken stock. Bring to a boil, reduce heat and simmer the mixture for 30 to 40 minutes until vegetables are tender. In a blender, purée mixture in batches. Return to saucepan, add herbs and corn and cook 5 minutes longer. Add salt and white pepper to taste.

Serves 6 to 8

Black Bean and Fresh Corn Salad

Fine-tasting and colorful, the textures and flavors of this inviting salad are splendid together.

> 2 cups cooked or canned black beans, drained
> 2 cups briefly cooked corn kernels, drained
> 2 tomatoes, peeled, seeded and diced
> ½ red bell pepper, diced
> ½ green bell pepper, diced
> 4 scallions, sliced
> 3 tablespoons minced cilantro
> 2 tablespoons red wine vinegar
> ½ teaspoon ground cumin
> ⅛ teaspoon red pepper flakes
> 3 tablespoons olive oil
> salt and freshly ground pepper to taste

GARNISH:
parsley or cilantro

Mix all the ingredients together about an hour before serving to blend flavors. Add salt and pepper to taste. Garnish and serve on lettuce as individual salads or as a colorful relish/salad with buffet dinners.

Makes 5 to 6 cups

Sopa de Maiz
Chile Corn Soup

*A very satisfying and rich-tasting soup
that will make any meal seem festive.*

**4 cups fresh corn
1 cup chicken stock
2 tablespoons butter
2 cups milk
¼ cup sugar
salt and white pepper to taste
2 tablespoons roasted and peeled
poblano or Anaheim chiles,
diced
24 tortilla chips
2 cups Monterey jack cheese,
cut into ½-inch cubes**

**GARNISH:
fresh cilantro or parsley**

Put the corn and chicken stock in a
blender or food processor. Blend just
long enough to break up the kernels.
Do not purée.

Put a fine sieve over a 4- or 5-quart
saucepan and strain the corn and
stock mixture, pressing with the
back of a wooden spoon to extract
as much liquid as possible. Discard
the squeezed-out corn kernels. Add
butter and simmer slowly 5 minutes,
stirring to keep the corn bits from
sticking. Add milk, sugar, salt and
pepper to taste. Add the chiles and
heat for another minute to blend
flavors.

To serve, place 3 or 4 broken
tortilla chips in the bottom of individual soup bowls. Heat soup slowly.
Add the cheese; when melted, serve
immediately. Garnish with cilantro
or parsley.

Serves 6

Light and Puffy
Corn Pudding

*A wonderful way to enjoy your harvest
when fresh corn on the cob starts to lose its
allure. Add 1 cup grated cheese to turn it
into a main-course meal.*

**4 eggs
2 cups fresh corn kernels
3 tablespoons all-purpose flour
1 tablespoon sugar
1 cup milk or cream
salt and freshly ground pepper
to taste**

Preheat oven to 325°F.

In a large bowl, beat the eggs
thoroughly. Add corn, mixing well.
Whisk the remaining ingredients
slowly into the egg and corn mixture.
Pour into a buttered 1½-quart
casserole. Bake for 1 hour 20 minutes
or until puffed and golden. A knife
inserted into the center should come
out clean. Serve hot.

Serves 4

CRESSES

A SPECIAL HINT

For those who do not tolerate raw onions in salads and/or are cutting down on salt, the "bite" of cresses provides an excellent, satisfying alternative.

WATERCRESS EGGDROP SOUP

A light and quickly prepared Chinese-style soup that really takes advantage of watercress' special flavor.

4 tablespoons chopped or ground pork (or use ground turkey)
2 tablespoons soy sauce
⅓ cup finely sliced celery—slice on diagonal
⅓ cup canned water chestnuts, drained and thinly sliced
2 scallions, thinly sliced
4 cups chicken stock
1 egg, beaten
1 cup chopped fresh broadleaf cress or watercress, packed
optional: ½ cup tofu, diced in ½-inch cubes

Combine meat with soy sauce and let them marinate briefly while cutting up vegetables. Bring stock to a boil and add the marinated meat. Reduce to a simmer and cook 5 minutes. Add all the prepared vegetables. Bring back to a boil and add beaten egg slowly in a steady stream so it forms thin ribbons. Remove from heat, stir and add watercress. Serve immediately.

Serves 4 to 6

CREAMY CRESS SALAD DRESSING

⅔ cup olive or other salad oil
2 cups tightly packed cress
6 scallions, finely chopped
½ teaspoon salt
1 teaspoon freshly ground pepper
4 tablespoons sour cream (or 2 tablespoons sour cream and 2 tablespoons very fresh plain yogurt)

Combine all ingredients except sour cream in a food processor, blender or bowl and mix well. With machine running (or using whisk if preparing by hand), slowly add sour cream, blending thoroughly. Refrigerate in airtight jar.

Makes about 1 cup

SWEET AND SOUR WATERCRESS SALAD

The mild peppery bite of watercress is perfectly balanced by the hint of spicy sweetness in the dressing.

DRESSING:
2 tablespoons lemon juice
¼ cup tarragon vinegar
¼ cup catsup
1 tablespoon plus 2 teaspoons sugar
½ teaspoon salt
1 teaspoon prepared mustard
1 teaspoon Worcestershire sauce
½ cup vegetable oil

SALAD INGREDIENTS:
2 large bunches of watercress, torn into bite-sized pieces and tough stems removed
large lettuce leaves to line individual salad plates

Whisk together all the dressing ingredients and toss a portion of the dressing with watercress leaves. (Reserve extra dressing for other salads.) Line each salad plate with a lettuce leaf and mound watercress salad in the center of each leaf to make individual salads.

Serves 6

CRESS LOVER'S SALAD

Serve this appetizing salad on individual plates. It looks especially pretty paired with sliced red ripe tomatoes.

2 cups cress (either watercress or curly cress), tough stems removed
1 large clove garlic
3 tablespoons good fruity olive oil
1½ tablespoons white wine vinegar
½ cup very finely grated Parmesan (don't use if too dried out—use only fresh, sweet cheese)
coarse salt to taste
freshly ground pepper to taste

Put the prepared cress in a serving bowl. Combine the garlic, oil and vinegar in a blender and process until the garlic is blended into the oil mixture. Toss the garlic dressing with the cress, then sprinkle on the Parmesan and toss well. Season to taste with salt and pepper.

Serves 2

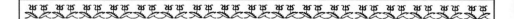

WALDORF CRESS SALAD

A tangy salad with the sweetness of apple and the bite of cress.

DRESSING:
¼ cup white wine vinegar
2 tablespoons lemon juice
½ teaspoon sugar
¾ teaspoon Dijon mustard
½ cup light olive or other
 salad oil

SALAD INGREDIENTS:
2 large, firm Red Delicious or
 other similar sweet red apples,
 cored and cut into ½-inch dice
⅓ cup Roquefort cheese,
 crumbled
⅓ cup coarsely chopped toasted
 walnuts
1 large bunch broadleaf cress
 or watercress, tough stems
 removed
½ head lettuce (preferably
 romaine) as first choice),
 torn into pieces

Combine dressing ingredients thoroughly. Toss apples, Roquefort cheese and walnuts in a small bowl and spoon 2 tablespoons of the dressing over the apple mixture. Mix well. To serve, add apple-cheese-nut mixture to cress and lettuce. Add 2 to 3 tablespoons more dressing and toss. Taste and add more dressing if desired.

Serves 4

CUCUMBERS

ISRAELI CUCUMBER SALAD

A creamy, crunchy and aromatic summer salad we think you'll make often. Great for Saturday supper after a full day.

> 4 scallions, cut into 1-inch
>   lengths
> ¼ teaspoon salt
> juice of one lemon, freshly
>   squeezed
> 1 large cucumber, peeled and
>   thinly sliced
> 1 bunch red radishes (8 to 10),
>   thinly sliced
> ½ cup sour cream (don't
>   substitute)
>
> GARNISH:
> 1 tablespoon chopped chives

Put the scallions and salt in a glass or wooden bowl, then use the edge and bottom of a heavy drinking glass to smash the scallions and salt thoroughly. Add the lemon juice and mix thoroughly. Add the cucumber and radishes; mix well. Add sour cream and mix well. Garnish with chopped chives and serve.

Serves 4

CHILLED CUCUMBER BORSCHT

Jewel-like colors and fresh full flavor give real meaning to the term "appetizer."

> 8 small peeled beets, cooked
>   until tender in water to cover;
>   reserve cooking water
> 2 scallions, chopped
> 1½ cups peeled, seeded and
>   chopped cucumbers
> 1 cup buttermilk
> 1 tablespoon red wine vinegar
> ⅛ teaspoon sugar
> 1½ teaspoons fresh lemon juice
> salt and pepper to taste
> 3 tablespoons finely chopped
>   fresh dill,
> 2 tablespoons finely chopped
>   fresh chives,

In a blender, purée the beets and water they were cooked in, scallion, half the cucumbers, and the buttermilk, vinegar, sugar and lemon juice. Add salt and pepper to taste. Transfer to a serving bowl. Add remaining cucumber and sprinkle with dill and chives. Serve chilled.

Serves 4

DANISH CUCUMBER SALAD

Made with fresh dill and sweet, crunchy cucumbers, this light salad is really addictive; it goes well with both light suppers and big buffet dinners in hot summer weather.

> 3 large cucumbers, peeled or
>   rinds scored
> salt
> ⅔ cup white vinegar
> ½ cup water
> ½ cup sugar
> ½ teaspoon salt
> ¼ teaspoon white pepper
> 2 tablespoons chopped fresh
>   dill or 1 tablespoon dried
>
> GARNISH:
> red or yellow cherry tomatoes

Slice cucumbers very thin. Arrange them in layers in a non-aluminum bowl, sprinkling each layer with salt. Put a plate on top of the cucumbers and a heavy weight over the dish. Let them remain at room temperature for several hours or overnight in the refrigerator.

Drain cucumbers thoroughly. Pat dry on paper towels. Return to the bowl. In a small skillet, heat to a boil the vinegar, water, sugar, salt and white pepper, stirring until the sugar is dissolved. Let the mixture cool to lukewarm, then pour over the cucumbers. Sprinkle with the chopped dill. Chill for 3 to 4 hours. Drain cucumbers and serve in a pretty glass bowl surrounded by cherry tomatoes.

Serves 6 to 8

CHINESE CUCUMBER SALAD

This delicate, well-balanced marinade shows off fresh cucumbers at their best.

> 3 cups thinly sliced cucumbers,
>   peeled or rinds scored
> ½ teaspoon salt
> ¼ teaspoon sugar
> 2 teaspoons white wine vinegar
>
> DRESSING:
> ½ teaspoon grated fresh ginger
> 1 teaspoon soy sauce
> ¼ teaspoon sugar
> 1 tablespoon white wine vinegar
> 2 tablespoons vegetable oil
> 1 tablespoon chopped chives
> 1 tablespoon chopped red bell
>   pepper
> ⅛ teaspoon red chile pepper
>   flakes
> salt and pepper to taste

Put cucumbers in a bowl with salt, sugar and vinegar. Toss and let stand 30 minutes. Drain, chill 30 minutes, and drain again. Combine dressing ingredients. Toss with drained cucumbers. Season with salt and pepper to taste.

Serves 4

GINGER-LIME CUCUMBER PICKLES WITH CINNAMON BASIL

2 pounds pickling-sized cucumbers, unpeeled
salt
1½ cups rice vinegar or plain white vinegar
1 cup sugar
5 tablespoons lime juice
1 cinnamon stick
6 whole cloves
2 tablespoons chopped fresh ginger
¼ cup chopped cinnamon basil

Halve cucumbers lengthwise; cut into 1-inch lengths. Put cucumbers in a colander. Sprinkle with salt. Allow to stand 30 minutes. Rinse off in cold water.

Combine remaining ingredients in a saucepan and bring to a boil, stirring until sugar is dissolved. Add cucumbers and simmer until they look glossy and transparent. With a slotted spoon, transfer cucumbers to sterilized jars. Boil down liquid until syrupy. Pour over cucumbers and allow to cool. Cover tightly, chill and store in refrigerator. Use within two weeks.

Makes about 1 quart

BOBBIE'S GARDEN GAZPACHO

A perfect recipe for using the food processor, but be careful not to over-chop the vegetables.

1 cup peeled and finely chopped tomatoes
½ cup finely chopped green peppers
½ cup finely chopped cucumbers
¼ cup finely chopped scallions
1 tablespoon chopped parsley
3 cloves garlic, minced
2 tablespoons minced chives
3 to 4 tablespoons tarragon vinegar
2 tablespoons olive oil (don't substitute unless you have to —olive oil tastes best here)
1 teaspoon salt
¼ teaspoon freshly ground pepper
1 teaspoon Worcestershire sauce
½ teaspoon Tabasco (or more to taste)
3 cups tomato juice

Combine all the ingredients in a glass or non-aluminum bowl and chill well.

Serves 4 to 8

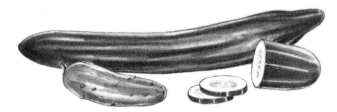

Rosamund's French Cornichons

Best made in small batches as they are picked. These tiny pickles are traditionally served with pâté. They go especially well with savories such as cold cuts and rye bread or crackers and cheese.

1¾ cups cornichon cucumbers,
  each no more than 1 ½ or
  2 inches
1½ tablespoons canning or
  pickling salt
2 small cloves garlic
2 three-inch sprigs fresh tarragon
  or one generous teaspoon dried
1½ cups mild white wine vinegar
2 cups water
2 teaspoons sugar

Clean cucumbers under running water; remove all stems and blossoms, being careful not to cut the ends of the cukes. In a small china or glass bowl, combine cucumbers, salt and just enough water to cover; let stand overnight at cool room temperature; drain.

Sterilize two half-pint canning jars; heat their caps and rings.

Put one garlic clove and a sprig of fresh tarragon in each drained hot jar. Pack with cucumbers.

In a small saucepan (not aluminum) heat the vinegar, the 2 cups of water and sugar to boiling over high heat. Cover cucumbers with this vinegar mixture and seal. Let flavors mature for two weeks before using them as an accompaniment to pâtés, cold cuts and savories of all kinds.

Makes 2 half-pint jars

Cucumber Gazpacho

This cool, refreshing and surprisingly filling first course or high-summer lunch is easily made using the blender. An admirable use of the abundant mid-summer cuke harvest.

1 large tomato, peeled
1 large or 2 medium cucumbers,
  peeled
½ green pepper
½ medium onion, chopped
¼ cup olive oil
¼ cup red wine vinegar
½ clove garlic
¼ teaspoon Tabasco sauce
½ teaspoon salt
¼ teaspoon fresh pepper
2 twelve-ounce cans tomato juice

GARNISHES:
1 large tomato, chopped
1 large cucumber, chopped
½ green pepper, chopped
1 cup fresh plain yogurt or
  lowfat sour cream

Put all the ingredients in the blender with half of the tomato juice. Purée thoroughly and then add and blend the other half of the juice. Chill for several hours to blend flavors. Serve cold and pass bowls of the garnishes.

Serves 4 to 6

EGGPLANT

BAKED GARLIC EGGPLANT

2 eggplants (or enough for 12
  one-inch slices)
4 tablespoons good olive oil
4 cloves garlic, each cut into
  6 slivers
salt and pepper to taste

GARNISH:
parsley

Preheat oven to 325°F.

Cut the eggplants into 12 one-inch slices. Oil two 13½ × 8¾-inch baking dishes with 1 tablespoon of oil each. Insert 2 slivers of garlic into each slice of eggplant and arrange eggplant slices in a single layer on the pans. Pour remaining oil over the eggplant. Season with salt and pepper. Bake 25 minutes. Sprinkle with parsley.

Serves 4 to 6

SWEET AND SOUR EGGPLANT

An easily prepared dish that really highlights the flavor of fresh-picked eggplants.

2 medium eggplants, sliced in
  ½-inch slices, then quartered
salt
2 tablespoons olive or other
  salad oil
optional: 1 small clove garlic,
  finely minced
2 tablespoons sugar
2 tablespoons red wine vinegar

Salt the eggplant slices and let them drain for 30 minutes, then rinse off and pat dry. Heat the oil in a large heavy skillet and add the eggplant (and garlic if used). Sauté until tender, 8 to 10 minutes. Sprinkle with the sugar, turn over the slices and continue to cook briefly until they begin to caramelize. Add the vinegar and stir to blend. Serve immediately.

Serves 4

BAKED EGGPLANT
WITH FETA CHEESE

An easy appetizer or whole meal for eggplant lovers.

**1 large or 2 medium eggplants
olive oil
⅓ cup feta cheese or Gorgonzola,
    if you love it
¼ cup finely chopped and packed
    fresh basil**

Preheat oven to 350°F.

Cut eggplant into ½-inch slices. Brush slices with olive oil and grill or broil until lightly browned on one side. Turn slices over and brush other side with oil. Arrange slices on an oiled baking sheet. Sprinkle the cheese over the slices. Bake 10 minutes or until cheese is bubbly and eggplant slices are soft. Sprinkle fresh chopped basil over the top of the eggplant slices and serve hot.

Serves 4 to 6

CRUNCHY
BROILED EGGPLANT

This is a delicious and fast way to enjoy fresh eggplant, and it doesn't use a lot of oil, as do so many eggplant recipes.

Slice an eggplant thin and spread each slice sparingly with mayonnaise. Then dip each slice in freshly grated Parmesan cheese, covering both sides. Arrange the slices on a non-stick or slightly oiled cookie sheet and broil them on each side just until they are golden brown and crunchy outside and soft and tender inside.

Serves 4

CAPONATA
Cold Eggplant Appetizer

A wonderful, rich-tasting appetizer, long part of traditional Italian cuisine and well worth making. Here is our version.

½ cup olive oil
1 large or 2 small eggplants (about 2 pounds) cut into 1-inch cubes
2 cloves garlic, minced
2 large onions, finely chopped
1 green or red bell pepper, seeded and chopped
3 cups peeled ripe tomatoes, cut into chunks
⅓ cup red wine vinegar
2 tablespoons sugar
2 tablespoons tomato sauce
½ cup green or black olives, cut in halves
3 tablespoons drained capers
⅓ cup finely chopped fresh basil, or 2 tablespoons dried
2 tablespoons chopped parsley
salt and pepper to taste
optional: 2 tablespoons slivered almonds or whole pine nuts

In a large heavy skillet, heat ¼ cup of the olive oil. Add eggplant cubes and sauté over medium–high heat, stirring and turning constantly for about 8 minutes, or until they are lightly browned. Remove to a bowl.

Pour the remaining ¼ cup of olive oil into the skillet, heat oil, add garlic, onion, and green pepper and sauté another 3 to 4 minutes or until softened. Add tomatoes and simmer 10 minutes over low heat, stirring frequently.

In a small saucepan, heat vinegar and sugar together over high heat until part of vinegar evaporates slightly, 2 to 3 minutes. Add to large skillet with onion mixture. Return eggplant to skillet along with tomato sauce, olives and capers and simmer uncovered, stirring frequently, for about 15 minutes. Stir in basil, parsley, salt and pepper to taste. Add a little extra vinegar if necessary. Stir in nuts if used and heat through for 5 minutes longer. Transfer to a serving dish. Stores very well in refrigerator.

Serve hot or cold with crackers.

Serves 12 to 14

Broiled
Turkish Eggplant

*A striking dish that makes a show-off
appetizer, first course or luncheon dish.*

>2 medium eggplants
>olive or other salad oil
>1 tablespoon butter
>1 large clove garlic, minced
>2 tablespoons chopped fresh basil
>3 to 4 ripe tomatoes, chopped
>½ teaspoon sugar
>salt to taste
>1 cup fresh plain yogurt or
>   sour cream

>GARNISH:
>chopped chives or scallions

Cut the eggplant into ½-inch slices.
Brush both sides of each slice with oil
and broil them on both sides until
soft and slightly browned. (Watch
closely as slices cook quickly!)

Prepare a simple tomato sauce: In
a heavy saucepan, melt butter and
add the minced garlic. Cook for
1 minute and add the basil and the
tomatoes. Stir and cook down until
they reach a fairly thick consistency.
Add the sugar, stir and remove from
heat; let cool slightly. Salt to taste.

On each plate, lay a slice of eggplant. Top with the tomato sauce but
leave the outer edges of each slice
showing—don't cover the slice completely. Finish by adding a generous
tablespoon of fresh yogurt or sour
cream in the center of the slice.
Sprinkle with chopped chives or
scallions.

Serves 8

Fennel

Fennel Braised
in Vermouth

*The aromatic braising liquid deepens
fennel's delicate flavor.*

>2 tablespoons olive oil
>1 small onion, finely chopped
>1 clove garlic, minced
>2 large bulbs fennel, sliced into
>   ½-inch slices
>¾ cup dry vermouth
>2 tablespoons minced leafy
>   fennel tops
>⅓ cup half-and-half or cream
>salt and pepper to taste
>½ cup freshly grated Parmesan
>   or Asiago cheese

Heat oil in a large deep skillet and
sauté onion and garlic until softened,
about 3 minutes. Add fennel and toss
until glazed. Add vermouth and
braise the fennel until tender-crisp
—about 8 minutes. Add the fennel
tops, the half-and-half, salt and pepper, and cook another 4 to 5 minutes
to reduce and slightly thicken the
sauce. Sprinkle with grated cheese;
serve immediately.

Serves 4

KALE

HEARTY PORTUGUESE KALE SOUP

On a cold and wet fall night, serve this soup with warm crusty bread and beer or red wine for a complete and satisfying hot meal.

1 tablespoon olive oil
½ pound of your favorite
 smoked sausage, sliced about
 ½ inch thick
4 cups chicken stock
1 medium onion, thinly sliced
3 medium potatoes, thinly sliced
1 large bunch kale (about
 1 pound), shredded
salt and pepper to taste

Heat the oil in a skillet and sauté the sausage just until the fat is rendered —3 to 5 minutes. Drain on paper towels and reserve. Bring the stock to a boil with the onion and the potatoes and simmer 10 to 15 minutes until the potatoes are very tender. Mash the onions and potatoes in the stock with a potato masher or slotted spoon. Add the drained sausage slices and the kale. Bring back to a boil and then simmer 4 to 6 minutes until the kale is tender. Taste for seasoning— depending on how spicy your sausage is, add salt and pepper to taste.

Serves 4 to 6

AUSTRIAN KALE

A traditional and delicious side dish for roast pork, beef or chicken.

2 bunches washed kale
1 clove garlic, minced
½ medium onion, coarsely
 chopped
2 tablespoons oil
1½ cups chicken stock or
 bouillon
4 medium potatoes, quartered
1 stalk chopped celery

GARNISH:
sour cream

Cut the kale leaves into ½-inch-wide strips. Blanch them in lightly salted boiling water for one minute. Set aside. Sauté the garlic and onion in the oil until lightly browned. Add the chicken stock, potatoes, celery, and blanched kale. Simmer together until potatoes fall apart and lose their shape. Stir; season with salt and pepper, garnish with sour cream and serve.

Serves 4 to 6

LEEKS

LEMONY LEEK SOUP

The subtle flavors of the lemon, herbs and leeks combine perfectly in this silky smooth soup. Makes a memorable first course or a complete lunch.

1 tablespoon butter or margarine
2 tablespoons vegetable oil
6 cups (about 6 to 8) thinly sliced leeks
1 carrot, thinly sliced
1 stalk celery, thinly sliced
6 cups chicken stock
1 tablespoon grated lemon zest (yellow part of peel)
2 tablespoons lemon juice
2 teaspoons fresh marjoram or 1 teaspoon dried
1 tablespoon chopped parsley
¼ cup rice
½ cup milk
salt and white pepper to taste

GARNISH:
sour cream or yogurt
3 tablespoons minced chives

In a 4- to 5-quart saucepan, heat butter and oil, add leeks, carrot and celery, and sauté until softened. Add chicken stock, lemon rind, lemon juice, marjoram, parsley and rice and simmer, covered, for about 40 minutes until vegetables are very tender. Purée in batches in a blender or food processor. Pour mixture back into saucepan; add milk, salt and white pepper to taste. If soup is too thick add extra milk or stock. Heat soup through, but do not boil. Serve hot or cold, sprinkled with chives and a dollop of sour cream or yogurt.

Serves 6 to 8

BRAISED AND GLAZED LEEKS

The succulent leeks braise slowly to perfection in this dish.

6 to 8 medium to large leeks
2 tablespoons olive oil
2 cloves garlic, minced
1 tablespoon water
1 teaspoon sugar
3 tablespoons white wine vinegar
salt and freshly ground pepper
2 tablespoons finely chopped parsley

Trim tops off leeks, leaving 1 inch of the green tops. Cut larger leeks into 1-inch slices, the smaller ones into 1½-inch pieces. In a large skillet, heat oil. Add garlic and sauté until softened. Add the leeks and toss to coat them with oil. Arrange the leeks in a single layer in a skillet. Add 1 tablespoon water. Cover pan and cook at very low heat for 20 to 25 minutes, shaking pan occasionally to keep them from sticking. When leeks are tender, turn up heat and sprinkle with sugar and vinegar. Stir gently until the leeks are glazed with the syrupy mixture. Season with salt and pepper; add parsley and serve.

Serves 4 to 6

LEEKS VICTOR

A new adaptation of a classic recipe for celery that works beautifully for leeks, enhancing their sweet and mild onion flavor.

DRESSING:
3 tablespoons fresh lemon juice
1 teaspoon Dijon mustard
⅛ teaspoon sugar
2 tablespoons chopped fresh parsley
2 tablespoons sweet pickle relish
¼ cup light olive oil
salt and pepper to taste

LEEKS:
4 to 6 leeks, ½ to ⅓ inch in
  diameter
2 to 3 cups rich chicken or beef stock
1 hard-boiled egg, finely chopped
optional but traditional: 1 two-
  ounce can anchovy fillets,
  drained and rinsed

Combine and blend all dressing ingredients. Set aside. Trim the leeks, leaving 2 inches of green leaves. Discard outer layer of leeks and cut off the root ends. Split each leek in half lengthwise; wash well. Place leeks in a deep skillet or saucepan large enough to hold them in one layer and cover with stock. Bring to a boil, then reduce heat and slowly simmer for about 15 minutes or until tender. With a slotted spoon, transfer leeks to a dish, again in a single layer. (Save the savory stock for another use.) Stir, then pour the dressing over the hot leeks; salt and pepper to taste. Allow the dish to cool and flavors to blend for at least several hours, basting occasionally. Top with chopped eggs and/or anchovy fillets, and serve as a side dish or on lettuce leaves as a salad.

Serves 4 to 6

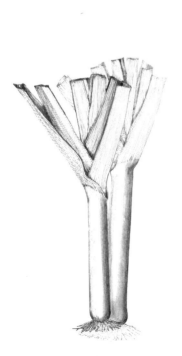

MELONS

MAMA SIMON'S PICKLED WATERMELON RIND

Our family recipe for this old-fashioned sweet pickle. Made from scratch,
it bears little resemblance to store-bought versions! Especially good to take on picnics.
Use like sweet pickles or chutney. Stores well in refrigerator.

7 pounds watermelon rind, leaving
on about ¼-inch pink flesh
1 tablespoon salt
6 lemons, washed
4 oranges, washed
3 cups white sugar
3 cups brown sugar
3 cinnamon sticks
6 whole peppercorns
4 teaspoons whole cloves
1 quart cider or other mild vinegar
1 cup water
½ pound candied ginger, chopped
fresh whole grape leaves, washed
and dried (this is the natural
way to keep pickles crispy)

Peel green outer layer from melon rind. Cut rind into 1- to 2-inch cubes. Put in a large saucepan, cover with cold water, add salt and bring to a boil, then turn down to a simmer and cook until the rind is tender but still crispy. Drain the rind and stop the cooking by dropping it into ice water. Drain and pat dry.

Squeeze the juice from the lemons and oranges and reserve. Cut their rinds into strips and remove pith.

Put rind strips in a pan. Cover with cold water, bring to a boil, then pour out the water. Repeat, boiling the rind for a total of 3 times. (Start with cold water each time.)

In a large saucepan, mix the sugars; add cinnamon, peppercorns, cloves, vinegar, water, ginger and lemon and orange juice. Heat, stirring, until sugar is dissolved. Cook about 30 minutes at medium heat or until reduced and slightly syrupy. Add reserved watermelon rind and lemon and orange rinds. Simmer gently for about 30 minutes or until the watermelon rind appears translucent.

Remove fruit with slotted spoon. Put a grape leaf in bottom of each jar and fill with rind, leaving 1 inch headroom. Cook remaining syrup down until slightly thickened, then pour over the rinds in the jars. Complete the seals if desired and process jars in hot-water bath for 20 minutes. Or store jars in refrigerator.

Makes 8 pints

MELON AND STRAWBERRIES WITH CRUNCHY STREUSEL TOPPING

A light, really scrumptious dessert. The fast run under the broiler seems to enhance the fresh fruits' flavor.

5 cups melon cubes, at room temperature
2 cups halved ripe strawberries, at room temperature
4 teaspoons orange juice
1 cup very fresh plain yogurt, drained

STREUSEL TOPPING:
½ cup cookie or graham cracker crumbs
½ cup dark brown sugar, packed
¼ cup all-purpose flour
2 pinches ground nutmeg
½ cup chopped walnuts or almonds
¼ cup butter

Preheat broiler. Spread the fruits in the bottom of a baking pan and sprinkle the orange juice evenly over them. Spread the yogurt evenly over the fruit in a thin layer. Combine Streusel Topping ingredients, adding butter last, and blend just until crumbly, but do not overmix. Sprinkle topping mixture over yogurt.

Run the pan under the preheated broiler for about 2 minutes, watching closely. Serve warm. Don't expect leftovers!

Serves 6

MELON MERINGUE

Light, elegant to serve and fun to make for a not-too-rich grand finale.

2 cantaloupes or Charentais melons, flesh cut into 1-inch cubes (or use a melon baller)
⅓ cup melon- or citrus-flavored liqueur
2 teaspoons grated orange rind
⅓ cup plus 1 tablespoon sugar
3 large egg whites at room temperature
¼ teaspoon cream of tartar
3 tablespoons sliced toasted almonds
2 tablespoons powdered sugar

Preheat oven to 500°F.

In a large baking dish or pretty ovenproof casserole, combine the melon with the liqueur, orange rind, and 1 tablespoon of the sugar and mix together gently but thoroughly. Let marinate for 15 to 30 minutes.

In a large bowl, beat the egg whites with an electric mixer on high speed. When they are foamy, add the cream of tartar and beat until soft peaks form. Gradually add the ⅓ cup of remaining granulated sugar and continue beating just until the whites hold stiff moist peaks. Spoon the beaten egg whites over the center of the melon pieces. Sprinkle evenly with nuts and powdered sugar. Bake only until the top is a light golden brown, about 4 or 5 minutes. Serve right away as a splendid dessert.

Serves 6

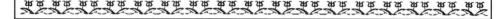

ONIONS

BREAD AND BUTTER PICKLED ONIONS

Mild, crunchy and especially good with cold cuts, cold chicken or tuna. Stores well in the refrigerator, too.

6 medium onions

BRINE MIXTURE:
1 cup white vinegar
2 quarts water
1 tablespoon salt

PICKLING MIXTURE:
2 cups white vinegar
2 cups sugar
1 tablespoon salt
3 tablespoons mustard seed
1 tablespoon celery seed
¼ teaspoon curry powder

Peel onions, cut in half crosswise, then into ¼-inch strips. Separate onions into strips and place in a bowl, covering with brine mixture. Let stand several hours or overnight.

In a 4- or 5-quart saucepan, combine pickling ingredients and bring to a boil over medium heat, stirring until sugar is dissolved. Boil 2 minutes. Remove the onion strips from the brine, draining well. Add them to the hot pickling mixture and boil for 1 minute. Pack the onions in 8 clean half-pint glass jars and cover them with the hot pickling mixture, leaving ½-inch headspace before sealing with 2-piece lids. Store in refrigerator for a week, allowing flavors to blend. (It stores well in the fridge.)

Makes about 8 half-pints

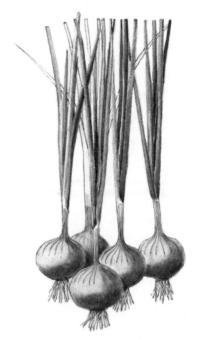

BAKED ONIONS

As good as baked potatoes and just as easy.

4 large whole onions, peeled
2 tablespoons softened butter
1 tablespoon fresh thyme or
** 1 teaspoon dried**
salt and pepper to taste

Preheat oven to 375°F.

Slice off and discard the top ½ inch of the stem end of each onion. Spread the cut surfaces with butter and sprinkle with thyme, salt and pepper. Place each onion on a square of foil, large enough to completely enclose it. Wrap each onion up tightly and put in preheated oven. Bake about 1 hour. Let each diner unwrap his or her own baked onion.

Serves 4

GRILLED SCALLIONS
OR BABY ONIONS

The sweet and mellow flavor of this dish is especially nice with our Red Beard scallions or Barletta baby onions. A fine accompaniment to grilled meats.

⅓ cup olive oil
1 large clove garlic, minced
1 teaspoon prepared mustard
½ teaspoon fresh ground pepper
salt to taste
16 half-inch-thick scallions, tops trimmed to 3 inches (or use baby onions)

Whisk together the oil, garlic, mustard, pepper and salt to make a marinade and pour over scallions in shallow pan. Marinate for several hours or as long as possible. Drain scallions. Grill over barbecue until soft and golden-brown. Transfer to a platter and serve at room temperature with grilled meats, poultry or vegetables.

Serves 4

BABY ONIONS
IN BASIL CREAM

This luxurious dish is great served over grilled fish, especially salmon. Or use it over brown or wild rice as a side dish.

1 pound baby onions
2 tablespoons butter
2 teaspoons shallots, finely chopped (or use scallions)
¼ cup fresh chopped basil
¼ cup dry vermouth
1 cup heavy cream
salt to taste

Cut the tops off the onions and discard. Put onions in boiling salted water for about 5 minutes. (If you have an abundance of chicken stock, poach them in it; they are tastier!)

Remove the onions. Cool. Take uncut end of onion and squeeze onion out the cut end. (You are removing the skins.) Reserve the onions.

In a skillet or sauté pan, heat the butter and sauté the shallots and basil. Deglaze the pan by adding the vermouth, bringing to a rapid boil for one minute and scraping up the bits with a spoon. Add cream. Simmer the sauce to reduce to desired consistency. Salt to taste. Add the onions and rewarm. Serve.

Serves 4 to 6

PEAS

GINGERED PEAS AND YELLOW SQUASH

Perfumed and colorful, this simple-to-fix recipe keeps intact the ingredients' fresh flavors and crisp textures.

    2 to 3 tablespoons oil
    3 tablespoons chopped fresh
      chives or scallions
    1 teaspoon garlic, minced
    2 teaspoons chopped fresh ginger
    1 pound sugar snap or snowpeas,
      stems and tips removed (strings
      pulled from sugar snaps)
    1 pound yellow summer squash,
      thinly sliced
    1 red bell pepper, chopped
    salt and pepper to taste
    2 tablespoons freshly chopped
      parsley (or 1 tablespoon
      chopped cilantro)

Heat oil in a wok or deep skillet. Sauté chives or scallions, garlic and ginger until sweet-smelling—about 1 minute. Add vegetables and stir-fry until tender-crisp—about 4 to 5 minutes. Add salt and pepper to taste. Sprinkle with parsley (or cilantro) and serve.

Serves 6 to 8

GARLICKY SNOWPEAS SAUTÉ

Crunchy and slightly Oriental tasting, this simple combination makes the peas really shine.

    2 tablespoons oil
    2 to 3 cloves garlic, depending
      on your taste, minced
    4 scallions, chopped
    1 large red, yellow or green bell
      pepper, diced or chopped
    1 pound fresh snowpeas, trimmed
    ½ cup jicama or water chestnuts,
      cubed
    2 teaspoons soy sauce

In a wok or deep skillet heat oil. Add garlic, scallions and bell pepper and sauté until softened and fragrant, about 1 minute. Add the snowpeas and jicama and sauté until cooked but still very tender-crisp, 2 to 3 minutes. Add soy sauce and toss together. Taste for seasoning, adding more soy sauce if desired.

Serves 4 to 6

INDONESIAN PILAF

A quickly made and evocative main dish. Part of the fun is to serve it with little bowls of as many of the different condiments as you have on hand.

PEANUT SAUCE:
⅓ cup creamy peanut butter
1 tablespoon dry sherry
2 tablespoons rice vinegar
2 teaspoons freshly grated ginger
⅛ teaspoon cayenne pepper
½ teaspoon sugar
1 clove garlic, minced
2 scallions, white part only,
   finely chopped (save tops)

RICE MIXTURE:
2 cups water
1 cup long grain white rice
2½ cups fresh peas (about
   2 pounds unshelled)
2 cups cooked chicken, cubed
½ cup chicken stock

GARNISH:
⅓ cup toasted chopped peanuts
reserved scallion tops, chopped

CONDIMENTS:
small bowls of chutney, sliced
   banana, raisins, coconut,
   cilantro, chopped orange,
   chopped apples, yogurt

In a saucepan, blend and stir together sauce ingredients, heating gently. Cover and keep warm. Boil water, add rice, cover tightly and reduce heat to a simmer for 15 minutes. Uncover and pour peas on top of rice, cover and simmer for another 5 minutes or until water is absorbed and rice and peas are tender. Mix in chicken. Transfer to a warm serving bowl. Toss rice mixture, chicken stock and reheated peanut sauce together. Top with peanuts and reserved chopped scallion tops. Serve with condiments.

Serves 6

CURRIED FRESH PEA SOUP

This smooth soup has a delicate, mild flavor that makes it a satisfying light lunch or supper completed with a green salad and fresh crispy bread.

3 tablespoons butter
2 cloves garlic, minced
2 onions, cut into ¼-inch slices
2 stalks celery, cut into ¼-inch
   slices
2 medium potatoes, cut into
   ¼-inch slices
1 carrot, cut into ⅛-inch slices
2½ cups fresh shelled peas
¼ teaspoon sugar
2 teaspoons curry powder
3 to 4 cups chicken stock
2 cups half-and-half or milk
salt and pepper to taste

GARNISH:
crisp bacon, finely chopped
chopped chives

In a saucepan melt butter, add garlic, onion, celery, potatoes and carrots, and sauté until softened. Add peas, sugar, curry and 2 cups of the chicken stock. Cover and simmer 15 to 20 minutes until vegetables are very tender.

Purée mixture in a blender one batch at a time. Pour back into the pot; add remaining chicken stock and enough milk or half-and-half to give the desired consistency. Heat through gently at low heat; do not boil. Taste for seasoning, adding salt and pepper as needed. Garnish each bowl with chopped crispy bacon and chives. The soup can be served either hot or cold.

Serves 6 to 8

PEAS À LA FRANÇAISE
Peas Braised with Heads of Lettuce

A traditional and succulent French dish for early peas and spring lettuce. In France this would be served as a separate course and eaten with a spoon as a special treat.

> 1½ firm heads Bibb lettuce,
>   7 to 8 inches in diameter
> 5 tablespoons butter
> ½ cup water
> 1 tablespoon sugar
> ½ teaspoon salt
> 3 cups fresh petits pois
> 5 parsley sprigs, tied together
>   with white string

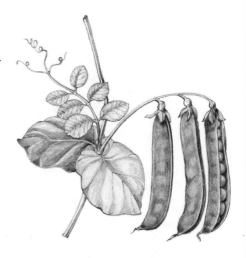

Wash the lettuce, remove any old leaves and cut into quarters. Wind several loops of kitchen string around each piece to hold it together when it cooks. In a heavy saucepan large enough to hold both lettuce and peas, heat 4 tablespoons of the butter, water, sugar and salt. Then add the peas and parsley. Place all the lettuce on top and with a baster dribble the liquid over it. Put a lid on the saucepan and bring to a boil. Turn heat to low and cook for about 10 minutes until the peas are tender, basting the lettuce from time to time. Discard the parsley and lettuce strings. Toss the peas and lettuce with the remaining 1 tablespoon of butter and serve at once.

Serves 4 as a first course or 6 as a vegetable dish.

PETIT POIS SALAD

This is a colorful side dish or picnic take-along that will please everyone's palate.

> 3½ cups petits pois or very
>   young peas, cooked in a little
>   water until tender, drained
>   and chilled
> 1 cup sour cream
> 2 scallions, finely chopped
> 6 slices bacon, cooked crisp,
>   drained and crumbled
> ½ teaspoon salt
> freshly ground pepper

Toss the peas with the rest of the ingredients and serve.

Serves 6 to 8

PEPPERS

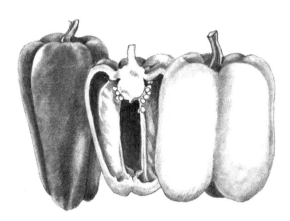

SWEET RED OR YELLOW PEPPER ESSENCE

Spoon this lovely sauce alongside green pesto sauce for a beautiful presentation.

4 to 6 red or yellow bell peppers
½ cup pine nuts
2 cloves garlic
½ cup olive oil
½ teaspoon salt
juice of 1 lemon

Roast, peel and seed the peppers. In a food processor or blender, grind pine nuts and garlic to a paste, then add peppers, oil, salt and lemon juice. Process until smooth. Use as a condiment with broiled chicken or fish, or cooked or raw sliced vegetables.

Makes about 2½ cups

COUNTRY-STYLE PEPPERS AND POTATOES

4 to 5 tablespoons oil
1 medium onion, very thinly sliced
2 cloves garlic, minced
4 medium to large boiling potatoes, cut into paper-thin pieces
2 red bell peppers, roasted, peeled, seeded and diced into 1-inch pieces
2 green bell peppers, roasted, peeled, seeded and diced into 1-inch pieces
2 tablespoons white wine vinegar
2 tablespoons chopped fresh basil
2 teaspoons finely chopped fresh tarragon,
½ teaspoon salt
¼ teaspoon freshly ground pepper

In a large heavy skillet, heat 4 tablespoons of oil. Add the onion, garlic and potato slices and sauté over low heat until fork-tender and lightly browned on both sides (add more oil if necessary). Add peppers, vinegar, fresh herbs, salt and pepper and toss together for several minutes. Taste for seasoning.

Serves 4 to 6

Mimi's Mexican Chicken Soup

This delicious, colorful soup with its clean citrusy flavor will especially please cilantro aficionados!

2 tablespoons vegetable or olive oil
1 onion, chopped
2 cloves garlic, minced
1 large red bell pepper, diced
1 quart chicken stock
⅓ cup fresh lime juice (most authentic and best) or ⅓ cup lemon juice
1 boneless cooked chicken breast half, shredded
1 cup cooked rice
1 cup chopped tomatoes
½ cup chopped fresh cilantro
salt and pepper to taste

GARNISH:
chopped fresh cilantro

In a large saucepan, heat oil and sauté onion, garlic and bell pepper until softened and fragrant—several minutes. Add the chicken stock and bring to a boil. Add the fresh lime or lemon juice, chicken meat and rice and bring back to a boil. Add tomatoes and cilantro, then turn off heat immediately. Taste and add salt and pepper if desired. Serve immediately with cilantro sprinkled over top as a garnish to each bowl.

Serves 4 to 6

Summer Garden Slaw

A new and colorful version of an old favorite for spicy food lovers.

DRESSING:
½ jalapeño or serrano or other small fresh hot chile, seeded and finely chopped
1 clove garlic, minced
2 tablespoons white wine vinegar
1 teaspoon sugar
1 teaspoon ground cumin
1 tablepoon chopped fresh oregano or ½ teaspoon dried
4 tablespoons olive oil
¼ teaspoon salt
generous pinch cayenne pepper

SLAW:
2 bell peppers, seeded and cut into thin strips (use several colors, if possible)
1 Anaheim or other mild chile, cut into very thin strips
1 small red onion, cut in half then into very fine strips
2 carrots, cut into very thin sticks, about as long as the pepper strips
½ head cabbage, finely cut or coarsely shredded
optional garnish:
1 tablespoon chopped cilantro

Combine and shake together all dressing ingredients. Combine the vegetables in a salad bowl and toss with the dressing. Let marinate at least ½ hour before serving. Garnish with cilantro.

Serves 4 to 6

Homemade Creole Sauce
with Chicken or Shrimp

*The ingredients of homemade Creole sauce go together quickly
and its rich flavor is unbeatable when prepared with the freshest ingredients.*

1 tablespoon butter
3 tablespoons vegetable oil
¼ cup all-purpose flour
1 large onion, coarsely chopped
2 stalks celery, cut into ½-inch
  slices
1 red bell pepper, cut into ½-inch
  dice
2 cloves garlic, minced
2 ½ pounds fresh tomatoes,
  peeled and coarsely chopped,
  including juice
1 eight-ounce can tomato sauce
1 teaspoon fresh thyme or
  ½ teaspoon dried
1 small bay leaf
½ teaspoon black pepper
pinch of red pepper flakes
¼ teaspoon Tabasco sauce
1 teaspoon brown sugar
1½ cups chicken stock
salt and cayenne pepper to taste
2 pounds peeled, deveined raw
  shrimp (or 4 chicken breast
  halves, skinned and boned,
  cut into bite-sized chunks)

GARNISH:
chopped parsley

In a large Dutch oven, stock pot or skillet, heat butter and 1 tablespoon of the oil; add flour and stir with a wooden spoon until flour turns golden brown. Remove the flour mixture from the pot and set aside. Heat 2 more tablespoons oil in the pot and add onion, celery, peppers and garlic. Sauté for about 3 to 5 minutes until softened. Add the reserved flour mixture and all the remaining ingredients except salt and cayenne. Bring to a boil. Reduce heat, cover and simmer for 30 to 40 minutes until softened. Season with the salt and cayenne to taste. Remove the bay leaf.

Just before serving, heat sauce to a simmer. If using shrimp: add raw shrimp and cook for 2 to 3 minutes, just until shrimp turns pink. If using chicken: add chicken chunks and cook 3 to 5 minutes or until done. You can also use a half-chicken and half-shrimp combination.

Serve hot Creole sauce over rice. Garnish with chopped parsley.

Makes 6 cups

64

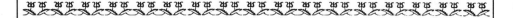

CHICKEN SANTA CRUZ

The aromatic, subtle flavors of this dish have drawn more raves than many other entrées we've prepared. Slow sautéing brings out the sweetness of the spices, herbs and onions and the rich mellow flavor of ripe peppers. Please do try it. Don't forget crusty French bread. By the way, leftovers make great sandwiches.

4 boneless chicken breast halves, skinned and cut into ½-inch strips
3 tablespoons lemon juice
4 large fresh bell peppers—use red, yellow, purple or deep green peppers (or any combination)
4 tablespoons vegetable or olive oil
2 cloves garlic, minced
2 large onions, finely sliced
2 teaspoons whole cumin seed or 1 teaspoon ground
2 teaspoons chopped fresh oregano or 1 teaspoon dried
2 teaspoons finely chopped fresh hot chile pepper or 1 teaspoon dried hot pepper flakes
½ teaspoon salt (or to taste)
¼ teaspoon freshly ground pepper
3 tablespoons finely chopped fresh parsley or chopped cilantro

Sprinkle chicken strips with lemon juice and set aside. Cut peppers in half and remove seeds and ribs. Cut into 1½-inch-wide strips. In a large skillet, heat the oil. Add garlic and cook one minute on moderate heat. Add the pepper strips, sliced onion, cumin, oregano and chile pepper. Stir the vegetables to coat evenly with oil. Cover and cook over medium heat for 10 minutes. Uncover pan, stir mixture, add chicken strips and stir to distribute them evenly in the vegetable mixture. Cover skillet again and cook gently for 10 more minutes. Uncover; chicken should be cooked through and vegetable mixture should be tender and very aromatic. Add salt and pepper to taste. Sprinkle with chopped parsley or cilantro and serve.

Serves 4 to 6

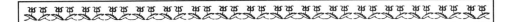

Stuffed Peppers Santa Cruz Style

An updated and delicious version of down-home comfort food that will please all comers!
Use several colors of peppers for best effect.

4 large green, red or yellow bell
  peppers
3 cups chicken stock
1 cup long grain rice
2 mild Italian sausages, casings
  removed
2 tablespoons olive oil
1 onion, chopped
½ red bell pepper, chopped
optional but delicious: ¼ cup
  chopped sun-dried tomatoes
1 Anaheim chile, roasted peeled,
  seeded and chopped (or use
  1 canned "California" mild
  green chile)
½ teaspoon celery seed
2 tablespoons lemon juice
½ cup chopped cilantro
salt and pepper to taste
Parmesan cheese

Preheat oven to 350°F.

Cut off the tops of the bell peppers and remove core and seeds. Cook in boiling salted water for 3 minutes to blanch. Remove from pan and turn upside-down to drain. Bring 2½ cups of the chicken stock to a boil (reserving remaining ½ cup), add rice, cover tightly and simmer for 20 minutes without removing the lid. In a large skillet, break up the sausage into small pieces. Sauté until lightly browned. Remove sausage and place on paper towels to drain. Heat olive oil in skillet, add onion, red pepper (and sun-dried tomatoes if used) and sauté until onion is translucent. Stir in rice, sausage, chile, celery seed, lemon juice, cilantro and reserved ½ cup chicken stock. Cook until thoroughly heated and liquid is absorbed. Add salt and pepper to taste. Stuff peppers with rice mixture. Arrange them side by side in a baking dish. Sprinkle tops with Parmesan cheese. Pour ½ cup boiling water around the peppers. Bake at 350°F for 30 to 35 minutes.

Serves 4

Bell Pepper Bounty

An aromatic and colorful salad to make in high pepper season.

3 tablespoons lemon juice
2 tablespoons minced fresh
   parsley
½ teaspoon ground cumin
1 teaspoon sugar
optional: 1 small clove garlic,
   minced
⅓ cup olive oil (or use your
   favorite salad oil)
2 red or purple bell peppers,
   thinly sliced into lengthwise
   strips
2 green or yellow bell peppers,
   thinly sliced into lengthwise
   strips
salt and pepper to taste

In a small bowl, combine the lemon juice, parsley, cumin, sugar and garlic if used. Add oil gradually, whisking until thoroughly blended. Put the sliced peppers in a serving bowl and pour the dressing over them, mixing it well with the peppers. Add salt and pepper to taste. Chill, covered, for about 1 hour before serving to let flavors blend.

Makes 1½ to 2 cups

Sweet Red Bell Pepper Soubise with Sage

Serve under baby vegetables, with roast chicken or over grilled fish. It's wonderful on pizza. Or simply spread on toast to serve as an appetizer.

½ cup butter
4 cups yellow onions, cut into
   chunks
2 tablespoons chopped fresh sage
4 red bell peppers, roasted,
   seeded and chopped

Melt butter. Sauté the onions in the butter very, very slowly until they are very soft, aromatic and deep golden-brown color. Be patient and stir often, letting them cook down gently.

Purée the onions, sage and roasted peppers in a blender or food processor until very smooth. Cool. Add salt and pepper to taste.

If you want a thinner purée, thin with half-and-half and adjust seasoning.

Serves 4 to 6

POTATOES

DILLY POTATO SALAD

Peas and potatoes in a creamy dressing with the bright flavor note of fresh dill.

**1½ pounds new potatoes,
   steamed and cut into chunks
1 cup cooked peas, drained
½ cup chopped celery**

**DRESSING:
¼ teaspoon salt
1 clove garlic, halved
2 tablespoons white wine vinegar
1 tablespoon Dijon mustard
½ teaspoon sugar
¼ cup mayonnaise
½ cup plain yogurt
6 scallions, finely sliced
6 tablespoons chopped fresh dill
freshly ground pepper to taste**

**GARNISH:
sprigs of fresh dill**

Prepare potatoes and peas and combine with celery. Set aside. Sprinkle salt in a pretty salad bowl. Rub garlic around bowl—discard garlic. Add vinegar, mustard, sugar, mayonnaise, yogurt, scallions and dill. Mix until combined. Add potatoes, peas and celery and freshly ground pepper to taste and mix together gently. Garnish with sprigs of dill.

Serves 6 to 8

ROASTED POTATOES WITH GARLIC AND HERBS

The aromas of roasting potatoes, herbs and garlic make this an irresistible dish.

**3 tablespoons olive oil
1 dozen small or 6 medium
   potatoes, washed but not
   peeled, cut into ½-inch slices
   and patted dry
½ to 1 head garlic (or to
   taste) separated into cloves
   and peeled
4 to 5 sprigs, 4 to 6 inches
   long, rosemary, thyme
   or basil**

Preheat oven to 400°F.

Spread olive oil in bottom of a 9 × 13-inch glass baking dish. Toss potato slices and garlic cloves in baking dish to coat with oil, then arrange in a single layer. Lay the sprigs of herbs on top of the potatoes. Cover the pan with foil or a cookie sheet and bake 20 minutes. Uncover and bake 15 to 20 minutes more or until potatoes are tender and begin to brown. Carefully remove herbs and discard. Serve immediately.

Serves 4

PUMPKINS

DRUNKEN APPLE-PUMPKIN PIE

A dramatic finish adds fun to this delectable dessert.

1 unbaked 9-inch pie shell
1 cup cooked pumpkin or winter
  squash, well drained
2 eggs
¾ cup firmly packed brown sugar
1 cup thick, chunky applesauce
1 tablespoon all-purpose flour
½ teaspoon salt
1 teaspoon cinnamon
1 teaspoon ginger
¼ teaspoon nutmeg
⅛ teaspoon allspice
⅛ teaspoon cloves
1½ cups half-and-half (or use
  1 twelve-ounce can evaporated
  milk)
1 teaspoon vanilla
1 cup pecan halves
2 tablespoons rum

Preheat oven to 425°F.

Chill pie shell until needed.

Mash pumpkin or squash. In a bowl, beat together the eggs and sugar until light. Mix in the pumpkin or winter squash, applesauce, flour, salt, cinnamon, ginger, nutmeg, allspice, cloves, half-and-half and vanilla and blend thoroughly. Pour into pie shell. Arrange pecan halves attractively over top of filling. Bake in the lower third of oven for 20 minutes, then reduce oven heat to 350°F and bake 30 to 35 minutes longer or until the filling is firm and a knife inserted 1 inch from the edge comes out clean. Cool on a wire rack. At serving time, warm rum in a small container suitable for pouring. Light the rum with a match and pour immediately while flaming over the pie. Serve with ice cream or whipped cream.

Serves 6 to 8

Pumpkin Cobbler

Everyone who tries this delicious dessert likes it better than ordinary pumpkin pie. The crust mixture rises to the top during baking to form a rich topping.

FILLING:
2 eggs, beaten
1 cup evaporated milk
3 cups cooked mashed pumpkin
   or butternut squash
1 cup white sugar
½ cup dark brown sugar
1 tablespoon all-purpose flour
1 teaspoon cinnamon
¼ teaspoon ginger
¼ teaspoon cloves
¼ teaspoon nutmeg
½ teaspoon salt

CRUST:
½ cup butter
1 cup all-purpose flour
1 cup white sugar
4 teaspoons baking powder
½ teaspoon salt
1 cup milk
1 teaspoon vanilla

TOPPING:
1 tablespoon butter
2 tablespoons white sugar

Preheat oven to 350°F.

In a large bowl, combine eggs, milk and pumpkin; add the rest of the filling ingredients, mix well and set aside. Then prepare the crust: melt the butter in a 9 × 11-inch baking pan. In another bowl, mix the remaining crust ingredients until just combined and pour into baking pan on top of the melted butter.
Spoon or slowly pour the filling evenly over the crust batter in the pan. Do not stir. Dot the top with the remaining 1 tablespoon butter and sprinkle with the 2 tablespoons sugar. Bake 1 hour.

Serves 8 to 10

HONEY-PUMPKIN BUTTER

This butter is smooth and rich-flavored but not too sweet or over-spicy. It is easy to make and tastes great on toast, muffins or pancakes.

> 2 cups cooked pumpkin, puréed
> ½ cup honey
> 1 teaspoon grated lemon rind
> 1 tablespoon lemon juice
> 1 teaspoon cinnamon
> ¼ teaspoon nutmeg
> ¼ teaspoon ginger
> ⅛ teaspoon cloves
> ¼ teaspoon salt

In a saucepan, combine all ingredients thoroughly. Simmer uncovered on low heat for 35 to 40 minutes, stirring frequently until quite thick—the same consistency as stiff apple butter. To check, drop a spoonful on a chilled saucer. When as thick as you like it, ladle into jelly jars and refrigerate.

Makes 1¼ to 1½ cups

PUMPKIN MUFFINS

Delicious with breakfast or as snacks.

> 2 cups unbleached all-purpose flour
> 2 teaspoons baking powder
> 1 tablespoon pumpkin pie spice mix
> ¼ teaspoon salt
> 2 eggs, slightly beaten
> 1 cup cooked mashed pumpkin, or winter squash, well drained
> ½ cup packed dark brown sugar
> 4 tablespoons melted butter
> ½ cup unsweetened applesauce
> ¼ cup milk, at room temperature

Preheat oven to 400°F.

Heavily grease a 12-cup muffin pan. Sift flour, baking powder, pumpkin pie spice and salt into a large bowl. In a separate bowl, beat together eggs, pumpkin, sugar, butter, applesauce and milk. Stir dry ingredients into the pumpkin mixture, just until they are combined—do not overmix. Spoon batter into muffin cups and bake until the muffins are golden, about 30 minutes. Serve warm or at room temperature.

Makes 1 dozen muffins

RADISHES

RADISH AND CUCUMBER SALAD

Combines two crunchy vegetables in an herb-scented, sweet-and-sour dressing.

- ¾ cup cider vinegar
- ¼ cup sugar
- 3 tablespoons chopped fresh dill
- 2 tablespoons chopped fresh parsley
- ¾ teaspoon mustard seed
- ¼ teaspoon each salt and pepper
- 3 large cucumbers, rinds scored and very thinly sliced
- 1 cup thinly sliced radishes

Combine vinegar, sugar, dill, parsley, mustard seed, salt and pepper; stir to dissolve sugar. Add cucumbers and let marinate in refrigerator for several hours. To serve: add the radishes and mix thoroughly.

Serves 6

CRUNCHY RADISHES WITH CREAMY SESAME DRESSING

This sesame dressing sets off the flavor of crispy radishes in a new and exotic fashion.

- 1½ cups thinly sliced radishes
- 1¾-inch length of daikon radish (if available), thinly sliced to matchstick size
- ¼ cup tahini (roasted sesame paste available at health and specialty food stores)
- 5 scallions, thinly sliced
- 3 tablespoons dry sherry
- 2 tablespoons lemon juice
- ¼ teaspoon each salt and sugar
- ¼ cup water
- optional: ⅓ cup chopped or sliced almonds; 1 cup cooked cubed chicken meat

Combine radishes in a bowl. For the dressing, stir the rest of the ingredients into the tahini; it will be a thick paste. Thin dressing to a creamy consistency with the water. Combine radishes with dressing and toss. Taste for seasoning. Sprinkle with chopped nuts if desired. Serve on lettuce. For a main-dish salad, mix in the almonds and chicken.

Serves 4

Salad Greens and Dressings

A Basic Herbed Salad Dressing for Salad Lovers

Be converted to making your own dressing!

   ¼ cup white wine vinegar
   1 to 2 tablespoons lemon juice
   (freshly squeezed is best)
   ½ teaspoon sugar
   ½ teaspoon mild prepared or
   Dijon mustard
   2 to 3 tablespoons freshly
   chopped herbs*
   ½ cup good light olive oil
   1 clove garlic, halved

Whisk all ingredients, except the garlic, thoroughly. Let the flavors blend at room temperature. Rub the salad bowl with the freshly cut halves of the garlic clove, then discard them. Add washed and dried assorted crispy greens. Pour over the whisked-up dressing, toss and serve promptly.

Serves 4 to 6

Good combinations are: equal parts basil, parsley, thyme and oregano, or equal parts basil, savory, thyme, or equal parts thyme, chives, basil.

Shepherd's Salad Dressing

Fine-quality ingredients turn this classically simple vinaigrette into the perfect companion for all fresh salads.

   ½ cup Shepherd's Ponente Extra
   Virgin Olive Oil (or another
   top quality light olive oil)
   ¼ cup Shepherd's Perseus
   Raspberry Vinegar (or
   another very fruity and not
   too tart raspberry vinegar)
   ½ teaspoon Dijon mustard
   ¼ teaspoon salt
   ½ to 1 clove fresh garlic, as
   you like

Combine all ingredients and shake to blend in a glass jar or whisk together thoroughly by hand. Before using, remove garlic clove.

Serves 6 to 8

MIXED FRESH GREENS WITH CURRIED DRESSING

2 quarts fresh assorted greens

DRESSING:
**2 tablespoons white wine vinegar
1 tablespoon vermouth
1 scant tablespoon Dijon mustard
1 tablespoon soy sauce
¼ teaspoon ground cumin
½ teaspoon curry powder
1 teaspoon sugar
¼ teaspoon freshly ground
  pepper
⅓ cup vegetable oil**

Wash, dry and tear greens into bite-sized pieces. Combine all dressing ingredients in a jar and shake well. Pour into salad bowl. Place greens in salad bowl on top of dressing but do not toss. Cover bowl tightly with plastic wrap and refrigerate for an hour or so. Just before serving, toss after adding any or all of the following:

**1 apple, diced
⅓ cup dry roasted peanuts
¼ cup golden raisins
4 scallions, chopped
1 tablespoon sesame seeds, toasted**

Serves 6

CALIFORNIA CITRUS SALAD

Light, crisp and very refreshing, the unusual combination of ingredients is a pure serendipity of colors and flavors.

**¼ cup fresh grapefruit juice
½ teaspoon sugar
¼ teaspoon salt
⅓ cup olive oil
3 grapefruits, peeled and
  sectioned, white
  membrane removed
1 large bunch red radishes,
  washed and thinly sliced
1 large head crispy Romaine,
  torn into pieces, or enough
  lettuce for 4 people
⅓ cup sunflower seeds, toasted**

In a small bowl, whisk together the grapefruit juice, sugar and salt. Add oil slowly in a stream, whisking the dressing until it is blended. In the salad bowl, combine the grapefruit sections, sliced radishes and lettuce. Add dressing and toss. Sprinkle the sunflower seeds over and serve.

Serves 4

Mixed Green Salad with "Hot Nuts and Bacon" Dressing

6 slices bacon, chopped
¼ cup chopped onion
2 tablespoons good-quality
olive oil
1 large clove garlic, minced
¼ teaspoon freshly ground
pepper
1 tablespoon mild vinegar
½ teaspoon freshly grated lemon
zest (yellow part of skin only)
1 tablespoon lemon juice
1 tablespoon chopped parsley
½ teaspoon finely chopped fresh
thyme or ¼ teaspoon dried
¼ teaspoon salt
2 teaspoons sugar
1½ quarts mixed salad greens:
several lettuces, arugula,
radicchio, a few leaves of
sorrel, etc.
⅓ cup toasted walnuts or
pecans, chopped
1 tablespoon chopped parsley

Cook the bacon until crisp in a skillet or wok and then drain, reserving 1½ tablespoons of the bacon fat in the pan. Heat the skillet again and add crumbled, drained bacon, onion, olive oil, garlic and pepper. Sauté until the onion is slightly softened —several minutes. Add the vinegar, lemon zest, lemon juice, parsley, thyme, salt and sugar. Cook another minute or 2 or until the onion is translucent. Add the mixed greens all at once and toss quickly over the heat until the leaves are coated with dressing and warmed but not really wilted—about 15 seconds. Taste and add more salt if desired. Then toss in the chopped nuts and sprinkle with chopped parsley. Serve right away.

Serves 6

Sweet and Sour Nutty Salad

The glazed crunchy nuts add something quite special and the other ingredients alternate between crispy and smooth, tart and sweet. We love it!

TOPPING:
2 tablespoons sugar
½ cup sliced almonds

DRESSING:
2 tablespoons white wine
vinegar
1 tablespoon lemon juice
¼ teaspoon salt
1 tablespoon sugar
⅓ cup vegetable oil
dash Tabasco sauce

SALAD INGREDIENTS:
1 head Romaine
½ head butter lettuce
½ cup thinly sliced celery
½ cup fresh bean sprouts
1 scallion, finely chopped
1 small can mandarin oranges,
drained
2 tablespoons chopped parsley

Place sugar in a heavy skillet over medium heat. Stir well just until it turns honey color (don't let it brown). Remove from heat, add almonds and stir until they are coated. Spoon onto a greased pan. Cool, break apart and reserve.

Combine all the dressing ingredients in a jar and blend.

Tear lettuce into bite-sized pieces. Combine in salad bowl with celery, bean sprouts, scallion and the mandarin orange. Toss with dressing and add parsley. Just before serving, sprinkle with glazed nuts.

Serves 6

Garden Bouquet Salad with Lemon-Herb Vinaigrette

DRESSING:
1 small scallion, finely chopped
1 teaspoon Dijon mustard
2 to 3 tablespoons lemon juice
1 tablespoon dry white wine
1 egg yolk
1 tablespoon minced parsley
1 tablespoon minced chive
  blossom florets or chopped
  chive leaves
¼ teaspoon salt
pinch of freshly ground pepper
¾ cup olive oil

With a whisk, combine all the ingredients except the oil. Slowly whisk in oil, beating continually until thoroughly blended. Taste for seasoning. Chill until ready to use.

SALAD INGREDIENTS:
2 heads radicchio (or red leaf
  lettuce as a second choice)
2 heads mâche
3 or 4 fresh sorrel leaves
2 small heads Bibb lettuce
12 to 14 leaves or 2 handfuls
  young arugula or watercress
¾ cup fresh green and purple
  basil leaves
½ cup calendula petals
¼ cup borage flowers

Wash and dry salad greens. Reserve 6 to 8 radicchio or red lettuce leaves. Tear remaining salad greens into bite-sized pieces and combine with basil leaves in center of salad bowl. Line outer edge with reserved radicchio or red lettuce leaves. Sprinkle with flowers around the outside border. Whisk dressing and pour over the salad after presenting it at the table.

Serves 6

Warm Shrimp Salad

An unusual and delicious first-course salad that tastes wonderfully extravagant.

DRESSING:
2 cloves garlic
2 shallots or 3 scallions,
  chopped
2 tablespoons fresh tarragon or
  2 teaspoons dried
2 tablespoons chopped fresh
  ginger
¼ cup lime juice
3 tablespoons red wine vinegar
1 tablespoon soy sauce
½ cup vegetable oil
1 tablespoon sesame oil
fresh pepper to taste

SALAD INGREDIENTS:
12 ounces medium raw shrimp,
  peeled and deveined
salad greens: two heads of
  lettuce, one green, one red
  leaf; one bunch of rocket salad
  or other greens to taste, torn
  into bite-sized pieces

Combine the dressing ingredients in a blender or food processor and mix until well blended. Marinate the shrimp in 2 tablespoons of the dressing for 30 minutes, reserving the remaining dressing.

Sauté the shrimp in their dressing marinade, stir-frying quickly, until they are pink, about 2 minutes. Arrange salad greens in large salad bowl and scatter the hot shrimp on top. Pour the remaining dressing over the salad. Toss well together and serve.

Serves 4 to 6

SPICY THAI VINAIGRETTE

Wonderful over crunchy lettuces.

1 small clove garlic, minced
¼ teaspoon finely chopped
  fresh ginger
3 tablespoons rice vinegar
1 teaspoon brown sugar
1 teaspoon soy sauce
¼ cup vegetable oil
½ teaspoon sesame oil
¼ teaspoon red pepper flakes
  or hot chile oil
optional: chopped red onions
  or mandarin oranges;
  sliced jicama

Combine all ingredients and mix
well. Pour over mixed lettuces,
toss and serve.

Serves 4 to 6

LEMON BASIL PESTO DRESSING

Especially for lemon lovers.

⅓ cup lemon basil leaves
1 small clove garlic, minced
½ teaspoon finely chopped fresh
  oregano or ¼ teaspoon dried
3 tablespoons olive oil
2 tablespoons vegetable oil
1½ tablespoons fresh lemon juice
¼ cup freshly grated Parmesan
  cheese
freshly ground pepper
optional: ¼ cup pine nuts

Combine ingredients in blender and
blend briefly to emulsify. Serve over
fresh lettuce.

Serves 2

GREEK STYLE ENDIVE SALAD

Nice with garlic bread and a no-nonsense burgundy.

1 head curly endive, torn
  into bite-sized pieces
2 to 3 large tomatoes, cut in
  eighths
1 green or red bell pepper, cored
  and cut into small pieces
1 cup sliced cucumber
1 small sweet onion, sliced and
  separated into rings
⅓ pound feta cheese, broken
  into ½-inch pieces
18 Greek or Italian olives

DRESSING:
¼ cup fresh lemon juice
¾ cup olive oil
3 teaspoons fresh oregano or
  1½ teaspoons dried

In a large salad bowl, layer the endive, tomatoes, pepper, cucumber, onion, cheese and olives. Cover and refrigerate to chill well.

To serve, whisk together the dressing ingredients and pour about ½ cup of the mixture over the salad. Toss lightly.

Serves 6

MEMORABLE WILTED LETTUCE SALAD

2 heads leaf or butter lettuce
8 slices very lean bacon, chopped
¼ cup vinegar
2 teaspoons water
2 teaspoons sugar
dash salt and pepper
1 egg, beaten

Shred the lettuce into a large bowl. Fry the bacon crisp, but do not drain. Add the vinegar, water, sugar, salt and pepper and the beaten egg to the pan. Cook, stirring just until the mixture has thickened. Pour the dressing over the lettuce and toss until the salad is wilted. Serve right away and stand back for applause.

Serves 4 to 6

PERFECT GREEN GODDESS DRESSING

1 clove garlic, chopped
1 tube anchovy paste
3 tablespoons chopped chives
  or scallions
1 tablespoon lemon juice
3 tablespoons tarragon wine
  vinegar
½ cup sour cream
½ cup mayonnaise
¼ cup chopped parsley
freshly ground pepper to taste

Combine all ingredients in blender and blend thoroughly. Outstanding on a salad of fresh Romaine with thinly sliced fresh mushrooms.

Makes about 1 cup

3-GREEN SALAD DRESSING

Healthy, delicious and quickly made in a blender.

>1 cup tightly packed spinach leaves
>¾ cup loosely packed parsley leaves
>3 tablespoons chopped fresh basil
>3 tablespoons lemon juice
>¼ cup herb or cider vinegar
>½ teaspoon salt
>½ teaspoon freshly ground pepper
>½ teaspoon ground cumin
>1 small clove garlic, minced
>½ cup olive oil

Combine all ingredients in blender and blend until smooth. Use over any of your favorite fresh green salads. This tasty dressing can be stored in a covered container in the refrigerator 2 to 3 weeks.

Makes about 3 cups

CREAMY RASPBERRY
LETTUCES

Elegant and rich-tasting, this dressing is very special with soft-leaved lettuces.

>3 tablespoons raspberry vinegar
>1 tablespoon sugar
>⅓ cup light olive oil
>1 tablespoon sour cream
>1 tablespoon Dijon mustard
>½ cup fresh or frozen and defrosted raspberries
>2 heads fresh Bibb or butter lettuce, torn into bite-sized pieces
>½ cup walnuts, toasted

Whisk together the vinegar, sugar, oil, sour cream, mustard and about half the berries. Put lettuce in salad bowl or on plates and top with nuts and reserved berries. Drizzle with whisked dressing and serve.

Serves 4 to 6

Fresh Orange Salad Dressing

The fresh orange flavor comes through in this light and refreshing dressing that really makes salad greens sing.

¼ cup mild vinegar
1 teaspoon freshly grated orange zest (orange part of peel)
⅓ cup freshly squeezed orange juice
1 tablespoon minced parsley
1 teaspoon sugar
¼ teaspoon Worcestershire sauce
¼ teaspoon salt
½ teaspoon paprika
½ cup salad oil

Combine ingredients and blend or shake together thoroughly.

Makes 1 ¼ cups

Sweet and Sour Roquefort Dressing

Perfect for big wedges of lettuce or assorted mixed greens.

⅓ cup olive oil
¼ teaspoon paprika
½ teaspoon dry mustard
½ teaspoon sugar
1 tablespoon herb vinegar
1 tablespoon lemon juice
1 tablespoon dry white wine
1 teaspoon Worcestershire sauce
2 tablespoons Roquefort cheese, crumbled
freshly ground pepper to taste

Combine ingredients and blend. Serve over lettuces and/or mixed greens.

Serves 4

Fresh Spinach Salad

Tender fresh spinach leaves, crispy sweet red apple and just a few bites of smoky bacon make this a salad to look forward to.

1 very large bunch of spinach (about 1 pound)
4 scallions, chopped
1 red-skinned apple, cored but not peeled and coarsely chopped
3 slices bacon, fried crisp, drained and patted dry, then crumbled

DRESSING (makes enough for several salads):
¼ cup honey
½ cup good red wine vinegar
1 cup olive or other salad oil
½ teaspoon salt
1 teaspoon ground black pepper
2 tablespoons Worcestershire sauce

Whisk the dressing ingredients together. Combine the salad ingredients, toss with desired amount of dressing and serve immediately.

Serves 4

Tarragon Ginger Dressing

This is a piquant, almost spicy dressing that is equally good used hot over greens or at room temperature over mixed lettuces.

> 1 tablespoon vegetable oil
> 1 small clove garlic, minced
> 2 tablespoons finely chopped scallions
> ½ cup chicken stock
> 2 tablespoons red wine vinegar
> 1 teaspoon finely grated ginger
> 2 tablespoons chopped fresh tarragon or 1 teaspoon dried
> 2 tablespoons olive oil
> salt and freshly ground pepper to taste

In a skillet, heat vegetable oil. Add garlic and scallions and sauté until softened. Add stock and boil until the liquid is reduced by half—about 3 to 4 minutes. Stir in vinegar and cook an additional 2 minutes. Transfer to a bowl. Add ginger and tarragon. Gradually whisk in the olive oil. Add salt and pepper to taste.

Serves 4 to 6

Sesame Salad Dressing

> 1 clove garlic, minced
> 2 tablespoons tahini (sesame seed paste)
> 1 teaspoon honey
> ¼ cup lemon juice
> ¾ teaspoon ground cumin
> ½ cup olive oil
> 2 tablespoons freshly chopped parsley
> ¼ teaspoon salt
> freshly ground pepper to taste

Mix all ingredients together in a blender and process until well combined. Taste for seasoning, adding more salt to taste. Serve over mixed salad greens.

Makes about 1 cup

Creamy Parsley Salad Dressing

> ½ cup salad oil
> ⅓ cup finely chopped fresh parsley leaves
> 3 scallions, finely chopped
> ½ teaspoon salt
> ½ teaspoon freshly ground black pepper
> 2 tablespoons sour cream (or fresh plain yogurt)

Combine all ingredients except sour cream in food processor, blender or bowl and mix well. With machine running (or using whisk if preparing by hand), slowly add sour cream, blending thoroughly. Refrigerate in an airtight jar.

Makes about 1 cup

Romaine Salad with Feta Dressing

The sweet, crunchy leaves of Romaine go especially well with the slight tang of feta cheese.

  2 tablespoons red wine vinegar
  1 tablespoon white wine
  2 ounces feta cheese
  ¼ cup olive oil
  salt and freshly ground pepper
    to taste
  1 head Romaine lettuce, torn
    into bite-sized pieces
  1 small cucumber, seeded
    and chopped
  2 tablespoons finely chopped
    parsley

In a bowl, combine vinegar, wine and cheese, and add the oil in a thin stream, whisking until it is blended. Add salt and pepper to taste. Combine lettuce and cucumber and toss with dressing. Sprinkle with parsley before serving.

Serves 4

Buttermilk Blue Cheese Dressing

Buttermilk dressing is low in fat, piquant and flavorful.

  ½ cup fresh buttermilk
  ¼ cup crumbled blue cheese
  1 tablespoon olive oil
  1 scallion, finely chopped
  2 tablespoons red wine vinegar
  2 tablespoons finely chopped
    parsley
  pinch of sugar
  salt and pepper to taste

Combine all ingredients and blend. Pour over salad greens, toss and serve.

Serves 6

Roasted Garlic Dressing

This dressing is delicious with any green salad and will make your salad course a real event. Roasting the garlic gives it a wonderfully mellow and sweet mild flavor.

  5 to 6 large cloves garlic, unpeeled
  ¼ cup olive oil
  2 medium tomatoes, chopped
    and drained
  2 tablespoons freshly squeezed
    lemon juice
  3 chopped scallions, white part
    only
  2 tablespoons any herb vinegar
    (or use wine vinegar)
  ⅓ cup finely chopped fresh
    basil

Preheat oven to 350°F.
  Brush the garlic cloves well with 1 teaspoon of the oil, reserving the remaining oil. Roast the oiled garlic cloves in a pan until golden and soft, about 10 to 15 minutes. Watch carefully so garlic does not get overbrown. Remove and cool. When cool enough to handle, peel the garlic and combine the pulp with the reserved oil and rest of the ingredients in a blender. Blend until smooth and use to dress any mixed green salad.

Makes about 1 cup

CRUNCHY RED AND GREEN SALAD

Lots of flavor and texture in this serious salad really rewards your mouth.

DRESSING:
1 scallion, finely chopped
½ teaspoon finely chopped
   fresh thyme
1 tablespoon finely chopped
   fresh parsley
1 teaspoon Dijon mustard
2 tablespoons white vinegar
1 tablespoon white wine
¼ cup light olive oil

SALAD INGREDIENTS:
½ to 1 head radicchio, broken
   in bite-sized pieces (use less
   if you don't like its tartness;
   more if you do)
2 heads young and tender
   curly endive, torn into bite-
   sized pieces
1 large green-skinned apple
   (Granny Smiths or Pippins are
   best), cut into ¼-inch slices

Combine dressing ingredients and mix well. In a large salad bowl, combine salad ingredients. Whisk dressing again and pour over salad. Toss and serve.

Serves 4

ISLAND SIN SALAD

Wickedly delicious.

DRESSING:
3 tablespoons lemon juice
2 tablespoons honey
4 teaspoons soy sauce
1½ teaspoons freshly grated
   ginger
1 small clove garlic, minced
large pinch white pepper
½ cup light vegetable oil

SALAD INGREDIENTS:
2 small heads lettuce, torn
   into bite-sized pieces
optional (but very good):
   ¼ cup chopped cilantro
1 large orange, peeled and
   cut into segments, or 1 can
   mandarin oranges, drained
¼ cup sunflower seeds, toasted

Combine dressing ingredients, whisking oil in thoroughly. Put lettuce in salad bowl, add cilantro if used and arrange orange slices over lettuce. Sprinkle the salad with sunflower seeds. Whisk the dressing again to be sure it is well combined. Pour over salad, toss and serve.

Serves 4 to 6

ARUGULA AND NECTARINE SALAD

Green, tangy arugula contrasts with luscious fresh nectarine slices, all set off by a delicate raspberry vinaigrette. A beautiful presentation and great flavor. You can substitute fresh pears or peaches if nectarines aren't available.

DRESSING:
3 tablespoons raspberry vinegar
1 teaspoon Dijon mustard
5 tablespoons olive or vegetable oil
pinch each of sugar, salt and pepper

SALAD INGREDIENTS:
4 cups torn arugula leaves
4 cups torn butter lettuce leaves
2 to 3 ripe nectarines, sliced
⅓ cup toasted walnuts

Combine dressing ingredients and mix together well. Arrange salad ingredients in bowl. Pour dressing over them. Sprinkle with walnuts at the table so diners can see how pretty the salad looks in its bowl.

Serves 6 to 8

WARM SPINACH SALAD WITH ARUGULA

The slightly spicy arugula and spinach are beautifully set off by the full-flavored mushroom dressing.

1 large bunch spinach (about 1 pound), torn into bite-sized pieces
2 cups arugula leaves
4 tablespoons olive oil
¾ pound mushrooms, sliced
4 scallions, sliced
4 tablespoons red wine vinegar
2 teaspoons sugar
salt and pepper to taste
⅓ cup pine nuts or walnuts, toasted
⅓ pound feta cheese, crumbled

Arrange spinach and arugula leaves in a salad bowl. Set aside. Heat oil in a medium skillet, add mushrooms and scallions and sauté until softened and mushrooms have released a little liquid. Add vinegar, sugar, salt and pepper, stirring until heated through. Pour the mixture over spinach and arugula. Sprinkle with nuts and feta cheese and serve.

Serves 4 to 6

Layered Greek Salad

This cool, colorful and appetite-pleasing layered salad is definitely something to look forward to on a hot and sultry summer day.

DRESSING:
1 clove garlic, minced
½ teaspoon salt
2 tablespoons lemon juice
3 tablespoons white wine vinegar
½ teaspoon ground cumin
½ cup olive oil
1 teaspoon chopped fresh oregano
  or ½ teaspoon dried
⅛ teaspoon freshly ground pepper

SEASONING MIXTURE:
1 bunch thinly sliced scallions,
  including tops
½ cup chopped fresh mint leaves
½ to ¾ cup quartered, pitted
  Greek olives to taste
½ pound crumbled feta cheese

SALAD INGREDIENTS:
2 large cucumbers, peeled and
  cut into ½-inch dice
1 red bell pepper, seeded and cut
  into ½-inch dice
1 green, yellow or orange bell
  pepper, seeded and cut into
  ½-inch dice
4 large tomatoes, seeded, cut into
  ½-inch dice and well drained

GARNISH:
chopped fresh parsley

Prepare the dressing by combining its ingredients and set aside. Combine seasoning ingredients in a small bowl. In a deep, large glass serving bowl, alternate a layer of each chopped raw vegetable with the seasoning mixture, beginning with the cucumbers, then peppers, and finally the tomatoes, so that each vegetable has a layer of seasoning mixture between it and the next vegetable. Whisk the dressing and pour it evenly over the salad. Garnish with chopped parsley and then refrigerate the salad for at least ½ hour to let the flavors blend. You can prepare this salad up to 8 hours ahead.

Serves 4 to 6

Honey-Herb Dressing for Poached Baby Vegetables

½ cup olive oil
½ cup vegetable oil
¼ cup fresh dill leaf
2 tablespoons honey
⅓ cup chopped fresh basil
¼ teaspoon pepper
1 teaspoon salt
1 teaspoon dry mustard
1 tablespoon Worcestershire sauce
⅓ cup vinegar
2 cloves garlic, minced

Combine all ingredients and shake together well. Let flavors blend. Use to dress hot poached baby vegetables which can then be served either hot or at room temperature.

Makes about 2 cups

Herb Mustard Vinaigrette Salad

This delicious dressing is perfect with all greens and terrific on ripe tomato slices.

1 clove garlic, halved
¼ teaspoon salt
2 teaspoons Dijon mustard
2 tablespoons lemon juice
1 tablespoon rice vinegar or other very mild vinegar
2 tablespoons white wine
6 tablespoons olive oil
1 pinch sugar
fresh ground pepper to taste
1 teaspoon chopped fresh herbs (your choice)
assorted fresh salad greens

In a salad bowl, rub the garlic into the salt. Add mustard, lemon juice, vinegar and wine. Whisk in the oil. Add sugar, pepper and herbs. Remove garlic. Whisk again. Add salad greens and toss.

Makes ⅔ cup dressing

Sorrel and Shallot Butter for Baby Vegetables

¼ cup unsalted softened butter
½ cup finely chopped sorrel leaves
1 tablespoon finely chopped shallots
1 clove garlic, minced
3 drops Tabasco sauce
salt to taste

Blend all the above together evenly. Put a small amount on top of each serving of your favorite cooked baby vegetables. Can also be used on top of steak or chicken breasts.

Makes about 1 cup

Bagna Cauda
Hot Dipping Sauce for Baby Vegetables

On a platter or in a basket, arrange washed, trimmed baby vegetables at room temperature—your choice.

DRESSING:
¼ cup butter
¼ cup olive oil
4 cloves garlic, minced
1 two-ounce can anchovy filets, drained and chopped

Heat butter and olive oil in a small skillet and sauté garlic and anchovies for 5 minutes over very low heat, stirring constantly. Transfer to a small warmed fondue or chafing dish kept warm over a candle or on a hot tray.

Diners enjoy dipping the vegetables in the piquant dressing using fondue forks or long toothpicks. Stir dressing frequently.

Makes about ⅔ cup

SPINACH

CRUSTLESS SPINACH PIE

The spinach mixture forms a crust of its own with a pizza-like filling that will please everyone.

**2 pounds fresh spinach, stalks
  removed**
salt to taste
2 teaspoons lemon juice
3 tablespoons sour cream
3 tablespoons butter
2 scallions, chopped
½ pound fresh sliced mushrooms
4 tomatoes, diced and well drained
1 large clove garlic, minced
**1 tablespoon fresh thyme or
  1 teaspoon dried**
2 tablespoons minced parsley
freshly ground pepper
**3 tablespoons Parmesan cheese,
  freshly grated**

Preheat oven to 400°F.

Wash spinach thoroughly. Without shaking the water off the leaves, place in a large pot over high heat. As the spinach steams, sprinkle with salt and mash the leaves with a wooden spoon. After 2 or 3 minutes, turn off the heat and leave until cool enough to handle. Take handfuls of spinach and squeeze out as much water as possible. Chop coarsely. Place in a bowl; sprinkle with lemon juice and mix in sour cream.

In a saucepan, melt 2 tablespoons of the butter, sauté scallions until soft, add mushrooms and sauté for 3 to 5 minutes. Add tomatoes and turn up heat, stirring so that the liquid cooks away. Add garlic, thyme and parsley and simmer 2 to 3 minutes longer.

Grease an 8- or 9-inch glass oven-proof pie plate. Spread part of the spinach over the bottom and the remaining portions up the sides as if forming a pie shell. In the center, spoon the mushroom-tomato mixture. Sprinkle with salt, pepper and Parmesan cheese. Dot with remaining butter. Bake 15 minutes. Serve in wedges, hot or at room temperature.

Serves 4 to 6

FLORENTINE BAKED EGGS

Wonderful for brunch or a light summer supper, with toasted English muffins.

1 cup cooked and very well
  drained chopped spinach
⅛ teaspoon (a pinch) nutmeg
salt and pepper to taste
½ cup heavy cream
3 tablespoons finely chopped
  fresh basil
8 drops Tabasco sauce
freshly ground white pepper
4 large eggs, at room temperature
½ cup grated Swiss cheese
2 tablespoons freshly grated
  Parmesan cheese
optional: cooked, chopped
  Canadian bacon

Preheat oven to 375°F.

Mix spinach with nutmeg and salt and pepper to taste. Butter 4 large custard cups or individual ramekins. Line each with a nest of ¼ cup spinach. Add Canadian bacon if desired. Mix together the cream, basil and Tabasco. Pour 1 tablespoon of cream mixture into the center of each spinach nest. Break an egg into each ramekin and top with another tablespoon of cream mixture. Sprinkle with a grind of pepper and divide cheeses over the tops.

Place ramekins into a baking dish and pour boiling water into the pan to come halfway up the side of the ramekins. Bake until eggs are set to your liking—about 10 to 12 minutes.

Serves 4

BAKED SPINACH GNOCCHI

An easy-to-make version of this classic Italian delicacy.

1 very large bunch spinach
1 cup lowfat ricotta cheese
1 cup freshly grated Parmesan
  or Asiago cheese
2 tablespoons chopped parsley
1 scallion, chopped
1 tablespoon lemon juice
1 egg yolk
2 tablespoons all-purpose flour
½ teaspoon freshly grated nutmeg
¼ teaspoon salt
¼ teaspoon white pepper
extra flour for shaping gnocchi
1 cup shredded mozzarella cheese

Preheat oven to 350°F.

Steam or cook spinach briefly until tender. Drain well and chop fine. You should have 1 generous cup. Thoroughly combine spinach, ricotta cheese, Parmesan, parsley, scallion, lemon juice, egg yolk, flour, nutmeg, salt and pepper. Shape the mixture into little logs about 2 inches long and 1 inch in diameter. If sticky, sprinkle them lightly with additional flour. Place on a waxed-paper-lined baking sheet.

Cook the gnocchi in batches by carefully dropping them a few at a time into a large pot of gently boiling water. When they are cooked they will rise to the top—this just takes several minutes. Transfer them with a slotted spoon to a greased baking dish, laying them side by side in a single layer. Sprinkle the mozzarella cheese over the top. Bake 10 minutes or until well heated through and lightly browned.

**Serves 2 or 3 as a main course or
4 to 6 as a first course**

Summer Squash

Fran's Blue-Ribbon Zucchini Relish

This relish uses up that overabundance of midsummer zucchini. A staple, especially in barbecue season, it really appeals to "meat and potatoes" types who usually won't even contemplate zucchini.

- **10 firm medium zucchini**
- **1 tablespoon salt**
- **2 onions, coarsely chopped**
- **1 green bell pepper, diced**
- **1 red bell pepper or pimiento, diced**
- **2 stalks celery, sliced**
- **2½ cups cider vinegar**
- **2 cloves garlic, minced**
- **1½ cups sugar**
- **1 tablespoon mustard seed**
- **½ teaspoon allspice**
- **1 teaspoon turmeric**
- **2 teaspoons celery seed**
- **½ teaspoon black pepper**

Wash zucchini well and remove and discard ends; coarsely chop and mix with salt. Let stand 5 hours or overnight. Drain, rinse in cold water and drain once more.

Place the other vegetables in a saucepan with drained zucchini, vinegar, garlic, sugar and spices. Mix through, then bring to a boil, reduce heat and simmer for 30 minutes, stirring occasionally. Spoon at once into hot sterilized jars and store in the fridge to use with hot dogs, hamburgers, etc.

Makes 6 half-pint jars

Zucchini with Walnuts

A great side dish with barbecue-grilled meats.

- **4 cups zucchini, thinly sliced**
- **⅓ cup sliced scallion tops**
- **2 tablespoons butter**
- **3 to 4 tablespoons dry sherry**
- **½ teaspoon salt**
- **⅓ cup coarsely chopped walnuts, toasted**

In a large saucepan, combine zucchini, scallions and butter. Cook over low heat for 5 minutes. Stir in sherry and salt, cover and cook over low heat 3 to 5 minutes more until zucchini is tender. Stir in walnuts and serve.

Serves 4 to 6

STUFFED HERBED ZUCCHINI

6 to 7 medium zucchini
1 small onion, chopped
1 large clove garlic, chopped
3 tablespoons butter
1 cup seasoned bread crumbs
¾ cup freshly grated Parmesan
cheese
4 teaspoons fresh sweet marjoram
¼ cup chopped fresh parsley
salt and pepper to taste
2 eggs, beaten

Preheat oven to 375°F.

Wash zucchini, cut off and discard ends and steam until just tender. Cool. Split lengthwise, scoop out pulp (set aside), turn upside down and drain slightly. Mash pulp or spin in blender. Sauté the onion and garlic in butter until softened. Add squash pulp, crumbs, ½ cup of the cheese, herbs and seasonings. Add eggs and cook until mixture thickens. Stuff into zucchini shells, top with remaining cheese and place in a buttered casserole. Bake until browned, about 25 minutes. Serve hot or at room temperature.

Serves 6 to 8

YELLOW SQUASH WITH BASIL, PEPPERONI AND PARMESAN

For a light supper or lunch with French bread and red wine.

1 tablespoon olive oil
1 tablespoon butter
5 to 6 small yellow squash, chopped into chunks, enough to make 2 cups
1 small onion, chopped
¼ cup finely chopped pepperoni sausage
¼ cup freshly grated Parmesan cheese
1 tablespoon finely chopped fresh basil

In a large skillet, heat the olive oil and butter together, then add the squash, cooking until they are just heated through. Remove the squash from the pan and reserve. Add the onion and pepperoni and cook until the pepperoni is crisp and the onion limp. Add the squash back into the pepperoni mixture, and cook until the squash is tender-crisp. Add the Parmesan and the fresh basil; stir and serve immediately.

Serves 2

ZUCCHINI AND BASIL PASTA SALAD

Excellent as a main dish or side dish with barbecued meats.
Makes wonderful picnic fare.

4 medium zucchini, very coarsely
   grated
1 teaspoon salt
2½ cups packed fresh basil leaves
½ cup olive oil
3 cloves garlic
¾ teaspoon chopped fresh oregano
   or ½ teaspoon dried
6 cups chicken stock
¾ pound orzo (rice-shaped pasta)
¼ cup fresh lemon juice
¼ cup freshly grated Parmesan,
   Asiago or hard Monterey jack
   cheese
3 tablespoons chopped parsley
salt and pepper to taste

Sprinkle zucchini with salt in a colander and toss. Let stand 20 minutes, stirring once or twice. Squeeze zucchini dry. Transfer to a large bowl. Blend basil, oil, garlic and oregano together well in food processor or blender. Add to zucchini; reserve.

Bring chicken stock to a boil in a large pot. Add orzo and reduce heat, cooking until orzo is just tender, about 10 to 12 minutes. Drain well. Stir the pasta into the zucchini. Add the lemon juice, grated cheese and parsley. Season to taste with salt and pepper.

Serve warm, at room temperature or chilled.

Serves 8

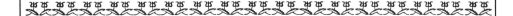

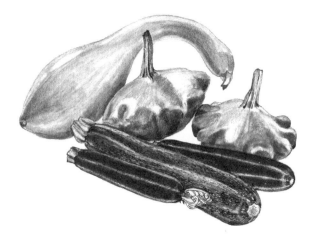

INDONESIAN ZUCCHINI SALAD/PICKLE

Serve with grilled meats and/or chicken as a salad or relish.

1 pound zucchini, cut into
  matchstick strips
1½ cups shredded cabbage
1 carrot, coarsely grated
1 tablespoon salt
1 onion, finely chopped
1 large clove garlic, minced
1 tablespoon finely chopped
  fresh ginger
2 tablespoons finely chopped
  peanuts or almonds
2 tablespoons vegetable oil
¼ teaspoon red pepper flakes
½ teaspoon ground turmeric
½ cup rice vinegar
1 tablespoon firmly packed
  brown sugar

GARNISH:
chopped peanuts
chopped cilantro or parsley

Sprinkle zucchini, cabbage and carrot with salt. Let stand several hours. Rinse in cold water; drain and pat dry and set aside. Combine the onion, garlic, ginger and peanuts and set aside.

In a large heavy skillet, heat oil, then add the onion mixture, pepper flakes and turmeric. Cook over moderately low heat, stirring frequently, for 5 to 8 minutes. Stir in vinegar and sugar and cook an additional 3 to 5 minutes or until slightly thickened. Add the drained zucchini, cabbage and carrot, stirring until coated with the mixture. Cool to room temperature. Chill for at least 2 hours before serving. Will keep covered in refrigerator for several weeks. Just before serving, garnish with peanuts and cilantro or parsley.

Makes about 4 cups

SUMMER SQUASH CHOWDER

A new combination of flavors enhances this light clam chowder.

- 2 tablespoons oil or butter
- 1 large onion, chopped
- 1 cup celery, chopped
- 4 to 5 medium yellow summer squash, sliced into 1-inch pieces
- 1 medium potato, cut into small cubes
- 1 tablespoon all-purpose flour
- 3 cups chicken stock
- 2 six-ounce cans chopped clams and their juice
- 1 ear fresh corn kernels or ¾ cup frozen corn
- 1 teaspoon fresh thyme or ½ teaspoon dried
- ⅛ teaspoon Tabasco sauce
- 1 tablespoon finely chopped fresh parsley
- 1 cup milk (lowfat or regular, not skim)
- 1 cup grated Cheddar cheese

Heat oil or butter in large saucepan. Add onion, celery, squash and potato and sauté for 5 minutes. Remove from heat. Sprinkle with the flour, stirring to coat vegetables. Add the chicken stock, bring to a boil and then lower heat and simmer, covered, for about 15 minutes or until vegetables are tender. Add the 2 cans of clams and their juice, the corn, thyme, Tabasco sauce and parsley. Return to a boil for 2 to 3 minutes. Reduce heat to a simmer. Add milk and cheese and heat through but do not boil. Stir well and serve piping hot.

Serves 4 to 6

GRILLED ZUCCHINI WITH FRESH ROSEMARY BUTTER

Delicious with squash, this tasty herb butter also goes perfectly with corn or green beans and is a tasty alternative to garlic butter on toasted French bread loaves. It freezes well, too.

ROSEMARY BUTTER:
- 2 scallions, white part only, finely chopped
- 2 tablespoons finely chopped fresh rosemary leaves
- ¼ teaspoon freshly ground pepper
- 1 teaspoon lemon juice
- ½ teaspoon finely grated lemon rind
- pinch ground cayenne pepper
- ½ cup salted butter, at room temperature

GRILLED ZUCCHINI:
- 6 medium zucchini
- olive oil

Thoroughly blend together the rosemary butter ingredients, then transfer to a deep custard cup or butter server, or place on a 12-inch-long roll of plastic wrap and roll into a 1-inch-thick log. Chill the herb butter slightly to firm and let flavors blend.

Slice zucchini lengthwise into thirds so you have long slices about ½ inch thick. Brush with olive oil. Grill or broil them until cooked and soft inside. Top each zucchini slice with a portion of the rosemary butter and serve.

Serves 3 to 4

VICKI SEBASTIANI'S RICOTTA-STUFFED SQUASH BLOSSOMS

A summer treat that shouldn't be missed.

12 to 15 fresh squash blossoms;
number used will vary
depending on size, so have
a few extra on hand.

FILLING:
1 pound ricotta cheese
1 medium onion, very finely
chopped
½ cup toasted almonds, finely
chopped
½ cup freshly grated Asiago
or Parmesan cheese
½ teaspoon ground pepper
1 teaspoon seasoning salt
2 tablespoons finely chopped
fresh basil
2 tablespoons finely chopped
parsley
2 tablespoons melted butter

Preheat oven to 350°F.

Mix all the filling ingredients together except the melted butter. Stuff squash blossoms carefully; don't overfill. Drizzle the melted butter over blossoms and bake for 15 minutes.

Serves 4

FRAN'S ZUCCHINI WITH PEANUT SAUCE

Quick and easy to make, this lavish-tasting dish will delight peanut lovers.

2 teaspoons vegetable oil
1 clove garlic, minced
1 teaspoon very finely chopped
fresh ginger
pinch of red pepper flakes
2 tablespoons oyster sauce
3 tablespoons rice vinegar
(don't substitute because rice
vinegar is very mild)
3 tablespoons chicken stock
¼ cup ground or very finely
chopped peanuts
pinch sugar
1 pound zucchini (about 5
medium), cut into 2- to
3-inch matchstick strips

In a large skillet, heat oil, add garlic, ginger and red pepper flakes and sauté until fragrant and softened—no more than 1 minute. Add oyster sauce, rice vinegar, chicken stock, ground peanuts and sugar. Add zucchini sticks and sauté, stirring often, just until zucchini are tender-crisp—3 to 5 minutes. Don't over-cook. Serve immediately as a hot dish, or at room temperature as a salad or take-along.

Serves 4 to 6

Fresh Zucchini Rellenos

A satisfying main dish with lots of color and flavor.

6 medium zucchini
1½ cups fresh corn kernels
   (use frozen and defrosted if
   fresh is unavailable)
2 eggs
2 tablespoons milk
¼ teaspoon salt
2 tablespoons chopped fresh
   Anaheim mild green chiles
   (or used canned mild green
   "California" chiles)
½ pound grated Cheddar cheese
2 tablespoons butter, at room
   temperature

TOMATO SAUCE:
4 large fresh tomatoes, chopped
   (or used 1 pound drained
   canned tomatoes)
⅓ cup chopped onions
2 cloves garlic, minced
¼ teaspoon salt
2 tablespoons olive oil
⅓ cup chopped fresh cilantro

In a blender, combine the tomatoes, onions, garlic and salt. Heat oil in a skillet. Add tomato mixture and heat about 15 minutes until thickened. Stir in cilantro.

Serves 4 to 6

Preheat oven to 350°F.

Cut zucchini in half lengthwise. Carefully scoop out the flesh and discard or save for another use. Place the zucchini shells in a greased shallow baking pan in a single layer. Combine the corn, eggs, milk and salt in a blender and blend to a coarse purée. Add chopped chiles. Mix 1½ cups of the grated cheese into the corn mixture. (Reserve ½ cup for topping.) Fill the zucchini shells with the corn mixture. Sprinkle with the remaining cheese. Dot with butter. Cover with foil and bake until tender, approximately 30 minutes. Do not overbake. Top with the freshly cooked tomato sauce.

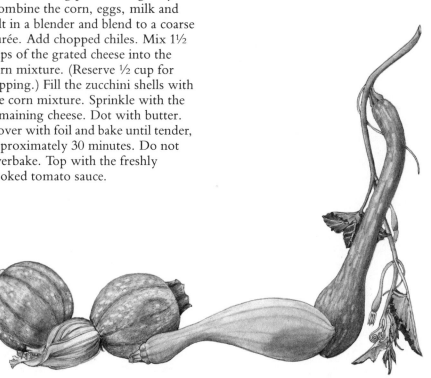

Zucchini Pancakes

Easy to make and very low in calories, these vegetable pancakes make a fine lunch or brunch dish.

6 medium zucchini
¾ teaspoon salt
1 tablespoon lemon juice
2 scallions, finely chopped
4 tablespoons finely chopped
  fresh basil or 2 tablespoons dried
2 small cloves garlic, minced
4 eggs, lightly beaten
2 tablespoons butter
2 tablespoons oil

Shred zucchini, sprinkle with salt and let stand for 5 to 10 minutes to draw off moisture. Squeeze or wring the shredded zucchini in a clean kitchen towel to remove all the moisture you can. Combine the squeezed-out zucchini with the rest of the ingredients except the butter and oil, mixing well. Heat the butter and oil in heavy skillet. Spoon the zucchini mixture into the heated skillet, shaping into pancakes. Cook over medium heat until set and light brown. Flip pancakes and finish cooking the other side.

Serve whole or cut into wedges. Sour cream or very fresh plain yogurt makes a nice accompaniment.

Serves 4

Ten Minute Zucchini Pizza

A surefire way for kids (of all ages) to enjoy zucchini

6 medium zucchini
olive oil
¾ cup pizza sauce
½ cup finely chopped basil
1¾ cup freshly grated
  mozzarella cheese
⅓ to ½ cup freshly grated
  Parmesan cheese

Preheat oven to 425°F.

Cut zucchini lengthwise into long ¼-inch slices. Pat dry and brush both sides with olive oil. Arrange side by side on an aluminum-foil-lined baking sheet or pizza pan. Bake 7 minutes or until just tender when pierced with a fork. Top generously with well-seasoned pizza sauce (any bottled kind you like is fine). Sprinkle with chopped fresh basil, freshly grated mozzarella and Parmesan cheese and put back into the oven for 2 to 3 minutes, until sauce is hot and bubbly and cheese is melted.

Serve immediately.

Serves 6

TOMATILLOS

GREEN GAZPACHO SALAD

Crunchy, cool and really refreshing.

**6 tomatillos, blanched in
    boiling water for 3 minutes,
    then coarsely chopped
1 clove garlic, minced
2 medium cucumbers, peeled,
    seeded and coarsely chopped
2 green bell peppers, seeded
    and coarsely chopped
4 scallions, coarsely chopped
1 green Anaheim chile,
    roasted, peeled, seeded
    and coarsely chopped
¼ cup chopped fresh parsley
2 tablespoons white wine vinegar
2 tablespoons olive oil
½ teaspoon Worcestershire sauce
⅛ teaspoon Tabasco sauce
½ teaspoon ground cumin
½ teaspoon salt
¼ teaspoon freshly ground
    pepper
4 ripe tomatoes cut into thick
    slices

GARNISH:
sour cream**

If using food processor to chop
vegetables, do not chop too fine.
Combine all ingredients except the
tomatoes. Mix well and then refrigerate for several hours to allow
flavors to blend. Taste for seasoning.
To serve, lay tomato slices on individual serving plates. Drain gazpacho
mixture and, using a slotted spoon,
spoon it on top of the tomato slices
on each plate. Garnish with a dollop
of sour cream if desired

Makes 5 to 6 cups

TOMATILLO DIP

*Makes an excellent dip, or serve along
with barbecued chicken or fish.*

**8 tomatillos, husked, roasted*
    and peeled
1 serrano chile, roasted,*
    peeled and seeded
1 small clove garlic
1 to 2 scallions, coarsely
    chopped
1 tablespoon lime juice
1 tablespoon chopped cilantro
salt and pepper to taste**

In a blender or food processor, combine all ingredients except cilantro.
Chop very coarsely; do not over-
process. Add cilantro and salt and
pepper to taste.

Makes about 1¼ cups

** To roast the tomatillos and chile, place
them on a grill or under the broiler and
turn them frequently until the skins char
and split. This gives them an extra
toasted, nutty flavor.*

TOMATOES

PASTA WITH FRESH CHILE PEPPER AND TOMATO SAUCE

For the very best flavor use our Italian plum tomatoes, if you've grown them; otherwise use small regular tomatoes.

12 ounces fresh or 8 ounces dried fettucine or linguini
⅓ cup good olive oil
10 Italian plum tomatoes, quartered
2 to 3 cloves garlic, minced
2 teaspoons fresh oregano or 1 teaspoon dried
1 to 2 small fresh chile peppers, remove seeds if desired, finely chopped
salt and pepper to taste
freshly grated Parmesan cheese

Cook the pasta in boiling salted water, timing it so it will be done just before it is mixed with the sauce. Heat the olive oil in a large skillet, then add the tomatoes, garlic, oregano, chile peppers, salt and pepper. Sauté over medium heat about 5 minutes or until tomatoes are softened but still hold their shape. In a warm bowl, combine sauce with hot drained pasta and toss together. Serve right away. Pass the Parmesan cheese.

Serves 3 to 4

TOMATO–LEMON CHUTNEY

An excellent chutney with a complex, not-too-sweet flavor. It makes a fine gift.

1 tablespoon oil
1 small whole fresh or dried chile chopped or crumbled
½ teaspoon cumin seed
¼ teaspoon nutmeg
¼ teaspoon mustard seed
4 large tomatoes, very thinly sliced
½ fresh lemon
⅓ cup raisins or currants
½ cup sugar

Heat oil in a saucepan. Add the crumbled chile, cumin seed, nutmeg and mustard seed. When the seeds start to jump in the oil, add the tomatoes.

Quarter the lemon half, removing any seeds, and lay it on top of the other ingredients in the pan. Simmer, stirring as needed to keep from sticking, for 15 minutes. Stir in the raisins or currants and the sugar. Continue to simmer, stirring frequently, until the mixture thickens, about 30 minutes. Cool and transfer to jars. Store chutney in the refrigerator.

Makes about 2 cups

Pasta with Fresh Tomatoes, Herbs and Garlic Sauce

Who wants to stand over a hot stove to enjoy fresh tomato-herb sauce? Try this recipe for a vividly colored, uncooked sauce that combines all the best summer flavors. Be sure to let the sauce stand for an hour before serving to blend all the flavors. A gardening cook's treasure.

**5 large ripe tomatoes, peeled, seeded and coarsely chopped
3 tablespoons chopped fresh sweet basil
1 tablespoon chopped fresh chives
3 tablespoons chopped Italian parsley
3 cloves garlic, minced
½ cup fruity olive oil
¾ cup finely grated mozzarella or fontina cheese
¼ teaspoon each salt and freshly ground pepper
12 ounces fresh or 8 ounces dried spaghetti or linguini
lots of freshly grated Parmesan cheese**

Have all the ingredients at room temperature. Prepare the sauce by combining tomatoes, basil, chives, parsley, garlic, olive oil, mozzarella cheese, salt and pepper. Let this sauce mixture stand at room temperature for about an hour to let the flavors blend. Cook and drain the pasta. In a warm bowl combine the hot drained pasta and the sauce. Toss together and serve right away. Pass the Parmesan cheese.

Serves 4

Tomato, Opal Basil and Mozzarella Salad

An alluring version of a very simple and traditional Italian dish.

**1 teaspoon lemon juice
2 tablespoons chopped purple opal basil
1 tablespoon chopped parsley
1 clove garlic, minced
2 tablespoons red wine vinegar
5 tablespoons olive oil
salt and freshly ground pepper to taste
fresh lettuce leaves
4 large tomatoes, sliced ¼ inch thick
8 ounces mozzarella cheese, thinly sliced
1 red onion, peeled and thinly sliced into rings**

**GARNISH:
sprigs of purple opal basil**

In of a blender or food processor, combine lemon juice, basil, parsley, garlic, vinegar and olive oil. Blend or process until smooth. Season with salt and pepper to taste.

Line a large serving dish with the lettuce leaves. Arrange alternating slices of tomato and mozzarella slices in rows, overlapping the slices a bit. Spoon the dressing over the salad. Sprinkle with black pepper; top with onion rings and garnish with sprigs of purple basil.

Serves 6

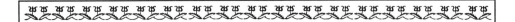

Sun-Dried Herb Tomatoes

Think of these as tomato "raisins" and use them anywhere you would like a strong, definitive tomato flavor: pastas, stews, etc. Also delicious as a colorful and savory addition to mixed green salads when first cut into thin strips.

**Italian plum tomatoes
salt
white vinegar
good Italian olive oil**

**ADDITIONS FOR EACH JAR:
2 cloves garlic
2 sprigs basil or rosemary**

Cut the tomatoes in half and cut out the stems. Lay them cut side up in one layer on trays and lightly salt them. Put them out in the sun and allow them to slowly dehydrate until they become shriveled and have the consistency of plump raisins. (Cover with cheesecloth or plastic screening to protect from insects.) Take the trays in at night if there is heavy dew. (Or use an electric dehydrator or a very low oven to dry the tomatoes.) After dehydrating, dip each dried tomato half in white vinegar, shaking off the excess vinegar. Place the tomatoes in clean, sterilized pint jars with garlic and your choice of herbs and cover completely with the olive oil. Store in the refrigerator but bring to room temperature before using.

Baked Stuffed Tomatoes

**8 medium or 4 large ripe
    tomatoes
salt and pepper to taste
2 cups cooked rice
1 cup loosely packed fresh
    parsley, chopped
1 cup loosely packed fresh
    basil, chopped
3 cloves garlic, finely minced
½ cup olive oil
¼ cup anchovy fillets,
    drained and mashed**

Preheat oven to 375°F.

Cut the tops off the tomatoes and scoop out the pulp, leaving a nice shell. Reserve tops and pulp. Sprinkle the shells with salt and pepper and let them drain upside down on paper towels.

In a large bowl, combine the cooked rice, parsley, basil, garlic, olive oil and anchovies. Press the reserved tomato pulp through a strainer to get ½ cup tomato juice and discard the pulp. Add the tomato juice to the rice mixture, blend well and season to taste.

Fill the tomatoes with stuffing, topping them with the reserved tops, and put them in a well-oiled shallow baking pan. Bake for 30 minutes. Serve at room temperature.

Serves 4 to 8

SALSA CRUDA

Nothing can substitute for freshly made salsa. Serve with chips, as a condiment, with grilled meat or poultry, or with rice and beans.

4 large tomatoes, peeled and
    cut into small dice
1 clove garlic, chopped
1 to 2 fresh jalapeño peppers,
    roasted, peeled, seeded and
    finely chopped
2 Anaheim or mild green chiles,
    roasted, peeled, seeded and
    finely chopped
6 scallions, finely chopped
1 tablespoon chopped parsley
½ teaspoon finely chopped
    fresh oregano, or ¼ teaspoon
    dried
2 tablespoons lime juice
1 tablespoon finely chopped
    fresh cilantro
pinch of sugar
salt and pepper to taste

Combine all the ingredients in a serving bowl. Season to taste with salt and pepper. Cover and set aside for several hours to allow flavors to blend. Before serving, drain off excess liquid.

Makes 3 to 4 cups

BAKED FRESH TOMATOES

This juicy herb-scented casserole is delicious as a lunch or as light supper fare.

8 to 9 medium ripe, fresh
    tomatoes
2 tablespoons minced onions
2 tablespoons finely chopped
    parsley
½ cup finely chopped fresh basil
2 tablespoons butter, cut into
    small pieces
¾ cup mozzarella cheese, cut
    into ½-inch cubes
¾ cup Cheddar cheese, cut
    into ½-inch cubes
¼ teaspoon each salt and freshly
    ground pepper
1½ cups seasoned bread croutons

Preheat oven to 375°.F

Dip tomatoes for about 15 seconds in very hot water to loosen skins. Remove skins and quarter tomatoes. Place in a saucepan and cook over medium heat for 3 minutes. Remove with a slotted spoon, reserving juice.

Grease a 2-quart casserole. Combine the tomatoes with onions, parsley, basil, butter, cheeses, salt, pepper and croutons in the casserole. Bake uncovered for 20 minutes. Serve hot or at room temperature.

Serves 4 to 6

FIRE AND ICE TOMATO SALAD

An old favorite that is perfect to serve with barbecued meals on a hot day.

6 large tomatoes, cut in thick wedges
1 large, green, red or yellow bell pepper, sliced in rings
1 large red onion, sliced in thin rings
1 cucumber, scored and thinly sliced

DRESSING:
½ cup vinegar
⅓ cup water
1 teaspoon celery seed
1½ teaspoons mustard seed
½ teaspoon salt
1 tablespoon sugar
dash of Tabasco sauce
⅛ teaspoon freshly ground pepper
1 tablespoon chopped parsley

OPTIONAL GARNISH:
1 avocado, cubed

Put the tomatoes, pepper and onions in alternate layers in a salad bowl, reserving cucumbers in a separate bowl. Combine dressing ingredients in a small saucepan. Bring to a boil and cook for 1 minute. Pour over vegetables. Chill. Just before serving, add the sliced cucumbers and sprinkle the parsley over the top of the vegetables.

Serves 6 to 8

GREEN TOMATO AND APPLE CHUTNEY

A fine way to use early- and late-season green tomatoes. This chutney keeps well and goes beautifully with cold meats, cheese or chicken.

5 cups coarsely chopped green tomatoes
3 cups peeled, cored and coarsely chopped apples (Pippins or Granny Smiths if available)
1 large red bell pepper, seeded and coarsely chopped
½ cup raisins
2 tablespoons finely chopped fresh ginger
2 cloves garlic, minced
½ teaspoon mustard seed
½ teaspoon ground cumin
1 teaspoon ground coriander
⅛ teaspoon nutmeg
⅛ teaspoon cayenne pepper
2 teaspoons salt
1 cup brown sugar, firmly packed
1 cup mild white or rice vinegar

In a large 4- or 5-quart saucepan, combine all ingredients. Bring to a boil and then simmer, stirring occasionally, for about 45 minutes or until mixture is thickened. Cool, then store in glass jars in the refrigerator or seal the jars and process in a hot-water bath for 10 minutes for half-pints and 15 minutes for pints. Let chutney mellow for a few days before serving.

Makes about 5 cups

Fresh Tomato Sauce Santa Fe

A delicious, fast sauce for a high-summer spaghetti dinner. Needs no cooking and retains the ingredients' beautiful colors and fresh flavors.

4 to 6 large tomatoes, peeled,
  seeded and coarsely chopped
1 red onion, minced
2 jalapeño peppers, stemmed,
  seeded and finely chopped
  (roasted and peeled first if
  you have time)
2 to 3 cloves garlic, minced
1 cup finely chopped fresh
  mint leaves
2 tablespoons olive oil
2 tablespoons red wine vinegar
1 teaspoon salt
freshly ground pepper to taste
8 ounces dried linguini or
  spaghetti
¾ cup freshly grated Parmesan
  or Asiago cheese

Combine vegetables and mint leaves in a large bowl. Mix together oil and vinegar and pour over vegetables. Salt and pepper to taste. Let stand at room temperature 30 minutes to 1 hour to mix and develop flavors. Cook linguini in boiling salted water, drain well and toss with fresh sauce. Serve immediately, passing the grated cheese.

Serves 4

Tuscan Pizza

The rich concentrated sauce based on vine-ripened tomatoes makes this pizza extra special.

2 tablespoons olive oil
1 clove garlic, minced
1 small onion, chopped
1 cup coarsely chopped tomatoes,
  including their juice
¼ cup finely chopped fresh basil
2 tablespoons chopped fresh
  parsley
1 teaspoon finely chopped fresh
  oregano
pinch each of salt, pepper and
  sugar
prepared pizza crust or
  English muffins
olive oil
½ cup finely shredded
  prosciutto or ham
½ cup grated mozzarella cheese
¼ cup freshly grated Parmesan
  or Asiago cheese

Preheat oven to 400°F.

In a small skillet, heat the oil, add garlic and onion and sauté several minutes until fragrant and softened. Add tomatoes, then cover and simmer for 5 minutes. Uncover; add fresh herbs and a pinch each of salt, pepper and sugar. Cook over high heat, stirring until liquid is absorbed. Brush ready-to-use pizza crust or English muffins lightly with oil, then spread the tomato sauce over the top(s). Sprinkle with the prosciutto and cheeses. Bake on upper rack of oven for 5 to 8 minutes until cheese is bubbly and serve immediately.

Serves 4 to 8

HERBS AND EDIBLE FLOWERS

*H*aving *easy access to the aromas and flavors of fresh herbs in abundance is one of the best rewards of being a kitchen gardener. Properly used, their bright perfumes excite and stimulate our senses of taste and smell.*

Edible flowers combine both the ornamental and edible and open up a whole new aspect of gardening and cooking for both the eye and the palate. They will add elegance to a new dish or a quick pick-me-up to the appearance and flavor of everyday cooking. A standard caution: only certain flowers are edible—pick and use only flowers we identify here or that you have personally verified to be edible from an authoritative source. Use only blossoms you know haven't been sprayed, as most chemicals registered strictly for ornamentals are toxic.

Over the last decade cooks have abandoned the traditional canons of using certain herbs only with certain foods. We invite you to do the same! Start out with time-honored pairings but then experiment. For example, rosemary is wonderful with traditional partners chicken and white wine, but a pinch of its pungent piney flavor also lends sparkle to a big bowl of slightly sweetened fresh strawberries. Use herbs with a subtle hand: it is better to begin with too little and add more to taste. Try to add herbs the last 5 to 10 minutes of cooking to preserve their volatile essential oils.

I personally have a long-standing love affair with basils. In our garden we grow twelve varieties of this wonderful rich and spicy herb, mildly peppery with a trace of mint and clove flavor. You'll find many recipes in these pages that focus on this favorite aromatic, used both as a flavor focus and as a subtle herbal highlight.

Preserve your harvests of basils and other herbs either by freezing in heavy-duty plastic bags or try microwave drying (see page 120). Store in a cool, dry place out of sunlight. Most importantly, locate your herb garden in an easily accessible place so you'll be motivated to harvest and use fresh herbs for everyday cooking.

ITALIAN GREEN BASILS

Aromatic fresh basil leaves are one of the most indispensable summer flavors for both gardeners and cooks. Basil is an easy-to-grow and vigorous herb, producing abundant fragrant harvests of leaves. It is delicious fresh and easy to freeze or dry for later enjoyment. We were delighted to discover that the many regions of Italy have developed very fine-flavored but distinctly different strains of sweet green basil. Use them for these recipes or use any green basil fresh from your garden or greengrocer.

CLASSIC FRESH PESTO SAUCE

One of the best ways to keep an abundant basil harvest. It can be frozen for later use, too!

> 3 cups loosely packed fresh basil
>   leaves
> ½ cup chopped fresh parsley
> 3 large cloves garlic (more if
>   you love it)
> ½ cup pine nuts or pecan meats
> 1 cup freshly grated Parmesan or
>   Asiago cheese (use fresh cheese)
> 1 teaspoon fresh oregano or
>   ½ teaspoon dried
> ½ teaspoon freshly ground
>   pepper (or to taste)
> ½ to ⅔ cup fruity olive oil
> salt to taste

Combine all the ingredients in a food processor or blender, adding enough olive oil to make a thick, smooth sauce. Add salt to taste. Add to hot pasta. Toss to combine and serve right away with fresh garlic bread and a crisp salad.

Makes about 2 cups (enough for 4 servings of pasta)

CREAMY PESTO-TOPPED FISH

Simple, succulent and delicious!

> 6 fillets firm white-fleshed fish
> 1 tablespoon lemon juice
> ¼ cup pesto sauce (see recipe
>   at left)
> 3 ounces cream cheese, softened
>
> TOPPING:
> ¼ cup each grated Parmesan
>   cheese and bread crumbs

Preheat oven to 400°F.
  Butter a 9 × 12-inch baking pan. Sprinkle fish pieces with lemon juice and place in pan. Combine pesto sauce and cream cheese thoroughly and spread on top of the fish pieces. Combine Parmesan cheese and bread crumbs and sprinkle over pesto. Bake 10 minutes or until the fish flakes easily with a fork.

Serves 6

Pesto Stuffed Tomatoes

Cook 1 cup orzo or other rice-shaped pasta according to package directions. Stir in ⅓ cup pesto sauce (see recipe p. 107). Fill 4 hollowed-out, medium tomatoes with mixture. Top with grated Parmesan cheese and bake at 375°F for 15 minutes. Serve hot with barbecued steaks or chicken.

Serves 4

Basil Butter

Use on cooked vegetables or pasta, or on top of poached eggs or fish.

½ cup butter, at room temperature
2 teaspoons lemon juice
1 tablespoon chopped fresh parsley
3 tablespoons chopped fresh basil
salt and pepper to taste

Cream the butter and beat in the lemon juice, a little at a time. Beat in the parsley and basil and season with salt and pepper. Serve in a serving dish or place on waxed paper and roll into a log. Chill overnight and slice to serve.

Makes ½ cup

Stuffed Brandied Mushrooms

1 pound large mushrooms
½ cup melted butter
2½ tablespoons butter
½ cup minced shallots or scallions
2 large mild Italian sausages
3 ounces cream cheese, softened
⅓ cup bread crumbs
½ cup finely chopped fresh basil
4 tablespoons brandy
salt and pepper to taste

GARNISH:
fresh basil leaves

Preheat oven to 375°F.

Wash the mushrooms, pat dry and remove stems. Finely chop stems. Squeeze in a towel to remove excess moisture; set aside. Dip each mushroom cap in the ½ cup melted butter, coating all sides and the cavity as well. Place the buttered caps on a baking sheet and set aside.

In a skillet, melt the 2½ tablespoons butter. Add chopped mushroom stems and shallots or scallions and sauté until the moisture has evaporated. Transfer to a bowl.

Remove casing from sausage. Place in a skillet over moderate heat. Crumble with a fork and sauté until browned. Drain off fat. Add to mushroom stems. Blend in cream cheese, bread crumbs, basil and brandy. Add salt and pepper to taste. Fill each mushroom cap with the mixture, mounding it.

Bake mushrooms for 10 minutes, watching them carefully to prevent scorching. Serve on a platter garnished with fresh basil leaves.

The filled, unbaked mushroom caps may be prepared one day ahead.

Makes 20 to 24 appetizers; serves 4 as a main course

BASIL PRESERVED IN PARMESAN CHEESE

This mixture can be used to flavor vegetable soups or, as a quick pasta sauce, just combine it with butter, garlic and fresh parsley. Delicious in anything that you want to have a taste of basil.

2 cups tightly packed basil leaves
1 cup freshly grated Parmesan
  or Asiago cheese
salt and pepper
olive oil

Very finely mince the basil leaves. Mix thoroughly in a bowl with the cheese.

Pour a fine sprinkle of salt and pepper in the bottom of a sterilized pint jar. Add a ½-inch layer of the basil-cheese mixture. Press down to ⅓ inch thick.

Add another thin sprinkle of salt and pepper and another layer of basil mixture. Continue packing the layers tightly until you have the jar full.

Top the jar with ¼ inch of olive oil. Seal and put in the refrigerator to use as needed. It will keep practically indefinitely. To keep the preserve from discoloring, add a little oil to the top of the jar each time you use it.

Makes about 1½ cups

ROMAN-STYLE STUFFED ARTICHOKES

This simple recipe shows off the flavor of artichokes beautifully while making a handsome and elegant presentation at the table.

STUFFING MIXTURE:
½ cup grated Parmesan cheese
½ cup fine bread crumbs
1 clove garlic, minced
2 tablespoons chopped fresh basil
2 tablespoons minced parsley
salt and pepper to taste

4 medium artichokes
juice of 1 large lemon
½ cup boiling water
¼ cup olive oil

GARNISH:
sprigs of fresh basil

Preheat oven to 350°F.

Mix together the stuffing ingredients and set aside.

Discard the stem and outer leaves of the artichokes and trim the tops. Parboil in a large pot of salted water to cover for 15 minutes. Drain upside down; cool.

Spread the artichoke leaves apart. Using a small spoon or non-aluminum melon ball scoop, scrape out the fuzzy inedible (choke) part of the artichoke. Sprinkle inside with lemon juice. Spoon the stuffing into the center of each artichoke and between the leaves.

Pour the ½ cup boiling water into a baking dish that will be just large enough to hold artichokes close together. Arrange artichokes right side up, side by side, in dish, and drizzle with the ¼ cup olive oil. Cover with foil. Bake artichokes for 1 hour, basting occasionally with additional olive oil. Serve warm; garnish with basil.

Serves 4

Marty's Basil-Rice Salad

A hearty and satisfying main dish salad for a hot day. This salad will also complement grilled meats and poultry nicely, or take it along to a barbecue picnic.

DRESSING:
2 tablespoons lemon juice
2 tablespoons red wine vinegar
¼ teaspoon each of salt and
   freshly ground pepper
2 tablespoons finely chopped
   fresh parsley
½ cup finely chopped fresh basil
1 clove garlic, minced
¼ cup plus 1 tablespoon olive oil

SALAD:
¼ cup finely chopped scallions
1½ cups cooked kidney beans
   or 1 can, drained
3 cups cooked rice
2 large carrots, shredded
2 tomatoes, halved and cut
   into thin slices

Mix together all the dressing ingredients.

Toss the scallions, beans, rice and carrots together. Mound evenly in a large serving bowl, then arrange tomato slices around the edge. Pour dressing evenly over salad and let the flavors blend for ½ hour. Serve either at room temperature or slightly chilled.

Serves 6 to 8

Sweet Pepper and Basil Stacks

Lovely to look at and eat. Makes a very successful and light first course or salad.

4 large red, yellow or orange
   bell peppers
4 large lettuce leaves
light olive oil
8 to 10 large fresh basil leaves
4 to 6 ounces feta or fresh
   chèvre cheese

Roast the peppers; put in plastic or paper bag. Cool 5 minutes. Skin, seed and cut in half lengthwise. Put lettuce leaves on individual salad plates. Lay a pepper half on each plate and drizzle with olive oil. Cover each pepper half with a layer of basil leaves, then thin slices of cheese. Drizzle with oil. Top with another pepper half and sprinkle on a little more oil to finish.

Serves 4

THAI CHICKEN WITH BASIL

Quick, spicy and delicious!

3 to 4 tablespoons seeded and
  finely chopped Anaheim or
  "California" green chiles
2 tablespoons soy sauce
1 teaspoon sugar
1 teaspoon vinegar
¾ cup chopped fresh basil leaves
2 tablespoons chopped fresh mint
½ teaspoon cornstarch
3 tablespoons vegetable oil
2 whole chicken breasts (1 pound
  each), boned, skinned, cut
  into strips 2 inches long by
  ¼ inch thick
2 cloves garlic, minced
1 large onion, halved, then
  sliced ¼ inch thick

Mix together chiles, soy sauce, sugar,
vinegar, basil, mint and cornstarch;
set aside.

Heat 2 tablespoons of the oil in a
large frying pan or wok over high
heat. When oil is hot, add chicken
and garlic. Cook, stirring constantly,
until meat loses its pinkness, about
4 minutes; turn out of pan and keep
warm.

Heat another tablespoon of oil in
pan, then add onion; cook, stirring,
for 2 minutes. Add chile mixture and
return chicken and juice to pan; cook,
stirring, until sauce thickens slightly.
Transfer to a serving platter and keep
warm. Serve with hot fluffy rice.

Serves 4 to 6

BUTTERFLIED BASIL SHRIMP

*Use as an appetizer or for luscious
individual salads.*

⅓ to ½ cup olive oil
1 large clove garlic, minced
½ cup packed fresh basil, finely
  chopped
3 tablespoons dry vermouth
3 tablespoons lemon juice
1 pound large raw shrimp,
  shelled and deveined, leaving
  tails on
salt and pepper to taste

GARNISH:
fresh lemon slices
whole fresh basil leaves

Heat oil over medium heat in a sauté
pan. Add garlic, chopped basil, vermouth and lemon juice. Butterfly the
shrimp along the inner curve, add to
the pan and sauté, stirring for 2 to 4
minutes—until they all turn pink.
Salt and pepper to taste. Transfer to
a bowl and chill to let flavors blend
for an hour or 2. Return to room
temperature to serve.

Skewer with garnishes to serve as
appetizers. Or, to serve as salads: line
four salad plates with soft lettuce
leaves, arrange shrimp and sauce on
top and garnish with the lemon slices
and basil leaves.

Serves 4 as an appetizer or salad

SCENTED BASILS

*A*mong our most popular specialty
varieties are the rare and scented basils:
lemon, opal, cinnamon and anise. All are
true basil varieties with the different flavor
characteristics their names describe. They
are easily grown, handsome plants in the
garden, and their intense scents make
them quite irresistible in the kitchen.

SCENTED BASIL VINEGAR

*This is our favorite way of enjoying the
flavors of scented basils year-round. If put
up in fall at the end of the basil season,
bottles make handsome holiday presents.
Anise and cinnamon basil vinegars are a
lovely soft pink color; opal basil is a deep
rich garnet; and lemon basil makes a
champagne-colored vinegar.*

Pack large 1-gallon plastic or glass
jars with rinsed and air-dried leaves
of any one of the scented basils.
(Stems and flowers are okay; no need
to separate leaves.) Fill up the jar
with plain white vinegar heated
almost to a boil. (White vinegar is
mildest and lets basil flavors come
through.) Cover with plastic wrap
and lid and allow to infuse for a
month or 2 in a cool place. Strain
vinegar through cheesecloth into
small decorative jars or clean wine
bottles and seal.

SCENTED BASIL VINEGAR CHICKEN

*An easy-to-prepare dinner dish with a
subtle taste and heavenly scent.*

> ¼ cup butter
> 1 large onion, finely chopped
> 4 chicken breast halves, skinned
> (and boned if desired)
> ½ cup any scented basil vinegar
> (see recipe at left)
> ¾ cup sour cream

Melt butter and sauté the onion until
soft and translucent. Add the chicken
breast pieces and sauté over low heat
until the chicken is done—no pink
shows when sliced. Remove the
chicken pieces to a warm serving dish
and keep warm. Add the basil vinegar
to the pan and simmer, stirring in all
the bits from the pan for about 5 minutes to reduce the sauce. Add the sour
cream, mix and heat through but do
not boil. Pour the sauce over the
chicken breasts and serve over fluffy
rice or noodles.

Serves 4

SCENTED BASIL JELLIES

These delicate jellies are unusual, delicious and easily made. Their clear jewel-like colors of rose pink, deep garnet and champagne are quite beautiful. You'll find they are delicious with cream cheese and crackers or bagels and they make wonderful presents for others—and yourself!

> 1½ cups packed fresh anise, cinnamon, opal or lemon basil
> 2 cups water
> 2 tablespoons rice vinegar
> pinch salt
> 3½ cups sugar
> 3 ounces liquid pectin

Wash and dry the basil in paper towels, then coarsely chop it. Put the basil in a large saucepan, and crush the leaves, using the bottom of a glass. Add the water, bring slowly to a boil and boil for 10 seconds. Remove the saucepan from the heat; cover and let sit for 15 minutes to steep.

Strain 1½ cups of liquid from the saucepan and pour through a fine strainer into another saucepan. Add the vinegar, salt and sugar and bring to a hard boil, stirring. When the boil can't be stirred down, add the pectin. Return to a hard boil that can't be stirred down and boil for exactly 1 minute, then remove saucepan from heat.

Skim off the foam and pour the hot jelly into 4 hot, sterilized half-pint jelly jars. Leave ½-inch headspace and seal at once with sterilized 2-piece lids, or melted paraffin.

Makes 4 cups

SCENTED BASIL HONEY

Chop the fresh leaves of one of the scented basils and wrap in a cheesecloth pouch. Add to a jar of mild honey. Cover jar and place in gently boiling water for 45 minutes. Remove from water and cool. Store about 10 days to let the flavors blend. Remove herb; strain if desired.

ANISE BASIL

ANISE BASIL BAKED FISH

Before baking or poaching fish steaks, thick fillets or whole fish, lay them on a bed of freshly picked anise basil. The herb will impart a subtle and delicious flavor in the cooking process. The anise basil can also be used when barbecuing fish: just tie a bunch together and use as a brush when basting the fish with butter or oil.

ANISE BASIL TOMATO SAUCE

Use anise basil in any tomato-sauce-based Italian dishes. You'll find it adds delicate flavors of both anise and fennel that enhance the tomato sauce in a particularly delicious way.

ANISE BASIL CHUTNEY

Good with pork and chicken or turkey.

    3½ cups mincemeat
    1½ cups drained and crushed
      pineapple
    1 teaspoon curry powder
    2 tablespoons cider vinegar
    1 cup tightly packed anise basil
      leaves, finely chopped

In a heavy saucepan, combine all
ingredients and bring to a boil. Lower
heat and simmer, uncovered, for
20 minutes or until thickened. Pour
into clean glass jars and refrigerate,
letting flavors blend for several hours.
Store in refrigerator.

Makes about 6 cups

MELAMBROSIA FRUIT

*A well-balanced and elegant combination
of flavors. A refreshing and satisfying
dessert after a rich meal.*

    ½ fresh pineapple, cut into
      1-inch cubes
    1 cantaloupe, cut into 1-inch
      cubes
    1 teaspoon lemon juice
    2 tablespoons honey
    2 teaspoons orange-flavored
      liqueur
    2 teaspoons finely minced
      fresh anise basil
    1 teaspoon finely minced
      fresh mint

Combine fruits in an attractive serving bowl. In a separate bowl, whisk
together the lemon juice, honey,
liqueur, anise basil and mint. Toss
with the fruit and serve.

Serves 6

CINNAMON BASIL

TIPSY CINNAMON BASIL CHUTNEY

*A delicious palette of flavors; makes a
wonderful gift, too!*

    2 cups sliced peaches or
      mangoes, fresh or frozen
    ½ cup canned water-packed,
      bite-sized pineapple chunks,
      drained
    1 small unpeeled orange,
      quartered, seeded, thinly sliced
    2 tablespoons lemon juice
    ¾ cup sugar
    2 tablespoons chopped
      cinnamon basil
    2 tablespoons light rum

In a saucepan, combine peaches,
pineapple, orange, lemon juice and
sugar. Mix well. Bring to boil, then
simmer, uncovered, over low heat
until thick (approximately 30 to
40 minutes). During the last 5 minutes of cooking, add cinnamon
basil. Remove from heat and stir
in rum. Spoon at once into hot
sterilized jars. Process the jars in
a boiling water bath for 15 minutes,
or store in refrigerator.

Makes 2 cups

PERSIAN MEATBALLS

*The mint and basil add a special flavor to this hearty main dish that
everyone will thoroughly enjoy served over rice or couscous.*

MEATBALLS:
2 slices bread
1 cup milk
1 pound lean ground lamb or beef
½ teaspoon each salt and pepper
1 tablespoon finely chopped fresh
  mint
2 teaspoons finely chopped
  cinnamon basil
1 clove garlic, finely chopped
1 teaspoon lemon juice
1 medium onion, finely chopped
2 tablespoons freshly grated
  Parmesan or Asiago cheese
¼ cup red wine
olive oil

SAUCE:
1 teaspoon all-purpose flour
1 eight-ounce can tomato sauce
2 tablespoons red wine
½ large or 1 small bay leaf

GARNISH:
1 tablespoon chopped fresh mint

Soak bread in a cup or so of milk
—enough to cover—until milk is
absorbed. Squeeze out excess, then
crumble soaked bread into small
pieces. Combine with all other
meatball ingredients and shape into
walnut-size balls. Chill. Heat oil in
large skillet. Brown meatballs evenly
and remove from pan. Drain fat.

Add the teaspoon of flour to pan
and mix in tomato sauce slowly.
Add wine and bay leaf and heat to
simmer. Transfer meatballs back to
pan; cook over low heat until done
to your liking. To serve, remove bay
leaf and garnish with chopped mint
before serving.

Serves 4 to 6

Cinnamon Basil
Chicken & Nut Spread

A wonderful spread for afternoon teas, receptions, or any time you want something special.

½ cup unsalted butter, softened
1 tablespoon honey
⅔ cup very finely chopped
  cooked white chicken meat
1 tablespoon finely chopped
  cinnamon basil leaves
6 tablespoons almonds, toasted
  and finely chopped
salt to taste

Blend softened butter and honey until smooth. Stir in chicken, cinnamon basil and almonds. Salt to taste. Serve on very thin slices of crustless white bread that have been quartered or cut into interesting shapes.

Makes approximately ¾ cup

Mulled
Cinnamon Basil Punch

A very fragrant and satisfying punch served either hot or cold.

4 cups apple juice
¼ cup sugar
⅓ cup cinnamon basil leaves
  or to taste
1 cinnamon stick
½ teaspoon whole cloves
2 limes, thinly sliced

Heat apple juice, sugar, cinnamon basil, cinnamon stick and cloves, stirring until mixture comes to a boil. Reduce heat, stir in limes and simmer 5 minutes. Strain into mugs and serve hot, or cool and serve over ice for a cold drink.

Makes approximately 4 cups

Apples Baked with
Orange Juice
& Cinnamon Basil

4 large baking applies
½ lemon
½ cup chopped and pitted dates
2 tablespoons raisins
1 tablespoon chopped
  cinnamon basil
zest of 1 large orange (orange
  part of peel)
juice of 4 to 5 oranges
additional fruit juice, if needed
sugar

Preheat oven to 350°F.

Core apples almost through. Pare a 1-inch strip of skin from around the top. Rub cut surfaces with lemon, dropping a few drops into the core. Combine dates, raisins and cinnamon basil and fill center of apples with mixture. Arrange apples in a baking dish just large enough to hold them. Cut zest into very fine strips. Squeeze orange juice; pour around apples, using enough to make about ½-inch of juice in the dish. Drop cut strips of orange zest into juices.

Bake, basting with juices every 10 or 15 minutes, for 50 minutes or until apples are tender when pierced with a knife.

Sprinkle with a little sugar and broil with surface of fruit 4 inches below heat. Baste with remaining syrup until glazed.

Best made ahead of time; serve at room temperature. A dollop of sour cream or fresh yogurt is a nice garnish.

Serves 4

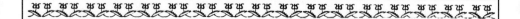

LEMON BASIL

LEMON BASIL HERBED RICE

2 tablespoons butter
3 tablespoons finely chopped
  onion
1 cup uncooked rice
¼ cup chopped lemon basil
1 small bay leaf
1 tablespoon chopped parsley
several drops Tabasco sauce
2½ cups chicken stock
salt and white pepper to taste

Preheat oven to 400°F.

Melt the butter in an ovenproof saucepan. Add the onion and cook until it is softened and translucent—about 5 minutes. Add the rice and cook, stirring, over medium heat for 3 minutes. Add lemon basil, the bay leaf, parsley, Tabasco and stock. Bring to boil, cover tightly and transfer to the oven. Bake 20 to 25 minutes or until rice is tender. Remove the bay leaf. Add salt and white pepper to taste. With a fork, fluff rice and serve.

Serves 3 to 4

CHICKEN SCALLOPINI À LA LEMON BASIL

4 chicken or turkey breast
  halves, skinned and boned
salt and freshly ground pepper
  to taste
2 tablespoons butter
2 tablespoons olive oil
½ cup dry white wine
1 tablespoon lemon juice
½ cup heavy cream
⅓ cup lemon basil leaves,
  finely chopped
½ teaspoon fresh thyme leaves
  or ¼ teaspoon dried
2 teaspoons minced fresh parsley

GARNISH:
lemon basil leaves
fresh lemon slices

Place chicken or turkey breasts between sheets of plastic wrap and pound with the edge of a mug or a wooden mallet evenly and gently until they are ¼ inch thick. Dredge each piece with salt and pepper. In a large skillet, heat butter and oil. When butter is melted, add the chicken and cook quickly for a minute or two on each side, or until it loses its pinkness inside. Remove chicken to a hot platter and keep warm in a 200°F oven.

Add the wine and lemon juice to the pan and cook over medium heat, stirring to blend in browned particles and juices. Boil until reduced by about half. Add the cream, lemon basil, thyme and parsley; boil until sauce thickens slightly. Pour any juices that collected on the chicken meat platter into the skillet. Taste sauce for seasoning, adding salt and pepper if needed. Pour sauce over the sautéed chicken and garnish with lemon basil leaves and lemon slices.

Serves 4

Lemon Basil Marinade for Grilled Fish or Chicken

⅓ cup lemon juice
2 teaspoons Dijon mustard
½ cup finely chopped fresh
   lemon basil
3 scallions, thinly sliced
2 tablespoons dry white wine
½ teaspoon salt
¼ teaspoon freshly ground
   pepper
1 cup olive oil

In a bowl combine all ingredients
except oil. Whisk in oil gradually
until mixture is thoroughly blended.
Marinate fish or chicken for 3 hours
or overnight before grilling.

Wonderful with foods cooked over
mesquite charcoal.

Makes 1½ cups

Fresh Fruits with Lemon Basil Dressing

*This recipe is good for both the eyes and
the appetite.*

Assemble four servings of the following combination of fruits:

grapefruit sections
orange sections
strawberries
kiwis, peeled and sliced
avocado, peeled and sliced

DRESSING:
2 tablespoons fresh lemon basil
   leaves, chopped
juice of ½ orange
juice of ½ lemon
juice of ½ lime
1 cup yogurt or sour cream
2 tablespoons honey

Prepare fruits and arrange on individual plates or a platter. Refrigerate.
In a blender or food processor, combine the lemon basil leaves with the
citrus juices. Process until puréed.
Add yogurt or sour cream and honey
and mix to blend. Taste and correct
seasonings with more citrus juice or
honey to suit your taste. Spoon dressing over fruits and serve.

Serves 4

CONFETTI RICE WITH TWO BASILS

A festive herbed rice that jazzes up any summer meal.

1 cup uncooked rice
**2 large ears fresh corn (or use
1 ten-ounce package frozen
corn, defrosted)**

**½ cup finely chopped celery
or fresh fennel**
¼ cup chopped purple opal basil
**1 red bell pepper or pimiento,
finely chopped**
2 tablespoons chopped parsley
salt and pepper to taste

VINAIGRETTE DRESSING:
2 scallions, finely chopped
3 tablespoons finely chopped basil
¼ cup lemon juice
⅓ cup olive oil
½ teaspoon salt
**¼ teaspoon freshly ground
pepper**

Cook rice in salted boiling water according to package directions. Do not overcook. Drain. Cook the fresh corn until tender. (For frozen corn, cook for two minutes, drain.) Cut corn kernels off cob and combine with rice. Combine vinaigrette dressing mixture in a jar. Shake well and pour over rice-corn mixture. Gently mix in celery or fennel, purple opal basil, red pepper and parsley. Season with additional salt and pepper to taste. Serve at room temperature.

Serves 6

CHEDDAR CRISPS

We haven't met anyone yet who didn't enjoy snacking on these. They make good appetizers, too.

8 ounces grated Cheddar cheese
**½ cup butter, at room
temperature**
½ teaspoon Tabasco sauce
½ teaspoon prepared mustard
1 cup all-purpose flour
**2 tablespoons chopped purple
opal basil**
1½ cup Rice Crispies cereal

Preheat oven to 350°F.

In a large bowl mix cheese, butter, Tabasco and mustard. Blend in flour and chopped opal basil. When combined, stir in Rice Crispies. Blend carefully and shape into small balls. Place on a greased baking sheet and flatted with the bottom of a lightly floured glass. Bake 15 minutes. Serve hot.

The crisps may be made several days ahead and stored in an airtight container or frozen. Reheat for 5 minutes when needed.

Makes 40

OTHER HERBS

MICROWAVE HERB DRYING

A quick and easy way to preserve fresh herbs.

Easy to do! Pick sprigs of fresh herbs and, if necessary, rinse and pat or air dry. Separate leaves from stems and measure 2 cups of leaves. Spread leaves evenly, in a thin layer, on a double thickness of paper towels. Microwave on high setting for a minimum of 4 and a maximum of 6 minutes. Check and stir the leaves several times during the drying process. When done, the herb leaves should be very brittle and quite crispy feeling when stirred with your fingers. (Note: the drying time may vary slightly depending on your individual microwave, so experiment the first few times, watching carefully so you do not overdry.) Let dried leaves cool completely and then store them whole or crumbled in airtight containers in a cool, dry place.

SHAKER HERB BLENDS

Here are some good herb combinations to have on hand at the table if you are trying to cut down on salt.

> **2 parts mild herbs, dried and crumbled; your choice of:**
> **basil**
> **summer savory**
> **lemon thyme**
> **dill**
> **parsley**
> **sweet marjoram**
> **1 part stronger herbs, dried and crumbled; your choice of:**
> **rosemary**
> **oregano**
> **sage**
> **Amsterdam cutting celery**

Whirl all the herbs in a blender or crumble together with your fingers. Keep on the table in a little bowl or a shaker with big holes. Optional additional seasoning: sesame seeds.

Compound Herb Butters

Keep on hand to dress up any plain grilled meat, chicken or fish, as an emergency sauce for pasta, to swirl into soups and stews, or to serve on hot breads.

**1 medium scallion, finely
   chopped
¼ cup packed fresh basil,
   parsley or cilantro leaves,
   finely chopped
1 tablespoon fresh lemon juice
¼ teaspoon salt
¼ teaspoon freshly ground
   white pepper
several drops hot pepper sauce
¼ teaspoon dry mustard
½ cup unsalted butter, softened**

Use a food processor to combine or mash together by hand the scallion and herbs. Add the lemon juice, salt and pepper, hot sauce, mustard and butter and mix together very thoroughly. Transfer to waxed paper or plastic wrap and roll into a log about 1 inch wide and 7 inches long. Freeze until ready to slice and use.

Makes about ½ cup

Herbed Bread Sticks

These simple-to-make appetizers are really delicious; we usually double the recipe so we can satisfy everyone's desire for more.

**1 small loaf white bread, thinly
   sliced
1 large clove garlic, chopped
¼ teaspoon salt
⅛ teaspoon pepper
2 tablespoons finely chopped
   fresh parsley
2 tablespoons finely chopped
   fresh chives
1 tablespoon fresh summer
   savory or sweet marjoram
   or 1 teaspoon dried
½ cup butter, softened
4 tablespoons freshly grated
   Parmesan cheese
melted butter**

Preheat oven to 350°F.

Trim the crusts from bread slices. Roll the bread slices flat with a rolling pin. Mash together the garlic, salt and pepper. Add the herbs and blend in the butter. Add cheese. Spread each slice of bread with the herb-butter mixture and roll up tightly, securing with toothpicks. Place on a baking sheet seam side down. Brush lightly with melted butter.

Bake 12 to 15 minutes until lightly browned, turning them several times while baking. Serve hot.

Makes 20 to 24

Old-Fashioned Herbed Chicken and Dumplings

A hearty one-dish meal that will please both gourmets and "just-plain-food" folks. The steaming, fluffy parsley dumplings make everyone happy!

1 three- to four-pound chicken, cut into serving pieces
3 whole cloves
8 to 12 baby onions, or 2 large onions, peeled and cut into quarters
4 to 6 carrots, peeled and cut into quarters
8 to 10 fresh mushrooms, cleaned
2 large cloves garlic, minced
1 teaspoon finely chopped fresh sweet marjoram
1 teaspoon finely chopped fresh thyme,
3 sprigs fresh parsley, chopped
2 teaspoons salt
1 teaspoon freshly ground pepper
1 cup dry white wine
1 cup sour cream (or ½ cup sour cream and ½ cup fresh plain yogurt)

DUMPLINGS:
1 cup biscuit mix
2 tablespoons freshly chopped parsley
6 tablespoons milk

Preheat oven to 375°F.

Butter a deep, ovenproof casserole dish that can also be put on stovetop burner.

Discard excess skin and fat from chicken pieces and place in casserole. Stick the cloves into 4 of the onion pieces. Add all vegetables, herbs and seasonings, and pour the wine over all. Cover the casserole and bake in oven until the chicken is just barely tender, about 35 to 45 minutes. *Do not overcook!*

To make dumplings, combine biscuit mix with chopped parsley. Stir in milk with fork until well moistened. Remove the casserole from the oven, stir in sour cream and place over medium heat on stovetop burner. When the chicken and vegetables are just bubbling, drop the dumplings from a teaspoon all around the edge of the casserole. Simmer 10 minutes uncovered and then 10 minutes covered.

Serve right away, giving each diner a generous portion of stew and several fluffy dumplings.

Serves 4 to 6

Herbed Flour

2 cups all-purpose flour
2 tablespoons minced dried herbs, a combination of several of the following: thyme, marjoram, savory, basil, dill, parsley
½ teaspoon salt
freshly ground pepper to taste

Combine all the ingredients and keep the herbed flour in a glass jar to use for dusting chicken or fish and for using in biscuits, quiche or pizza crusts, crêpe batter or herb breads and muffins. For longer storage, keep the jar in the refrigerator.

Makes 2 cups

GOLDEN BROWN CHIVE ROAST POTATOES

These crispy browned potatoes end up in handsome accordion shapes.

> **6 large baking potatoes**
> **¼ cup butter, melted**
> **½ teaspoon salt**
> **4 tablespoons freshly chopped chives**
> **½ cup your favorite shredded or grated cheese**
> **3 tablespoons bread crumbs**

Preheat oven to 350°F.

Peel potatoes and place in a bowl of cold water until ready to use. Dry thoroughly and cut a thin slice off the long side of each potato so it can sit flat. With a sharp knife, cut vertical slits from the top almost through to the bottom of each potato, being careful not to cut it through. Make slits ¼ to ½ inch apart.

Dip the slitted potatoes in melted butter and sprinkle with salt. Bake on a foil-covered baking sheet for 1 ½ hours, basting with the remaining butter. The potatoes will turn a crisp golden brown and the slits will open in accordion fashion as they bake. In the last 15 minutes, combine the chives, cheese and bread crumbs and stuff them into the slits in the potatoes, to form a delicious topping. Serve immediately and expect the diners to ignore everything else on their plates.

Serves 6

FRESH CILANTRO SALSA

> **2 jalapeño chiles, roasted, peeled, stems removed (leave seeds in if you like it very hot!)**
> **4 cloves garlic**
> **½ cup chopped red bell pepper**
> **1 medium red onion, coarsely chopped**
> **1 cup lightly packed cilantro leaves**
> **½ teaspoon cumin seed, toasted and ground**
> **1 tablespoon lime juice**
> **2 tablespoons red wine vinegar**
> **½ teaspoon salt**
> **2 tomatoes, quartered, seeded and drained**

In a food processor or by hand, mince the jalapeño chiles and garlic. Add the remaining ingredients except tomatoes, and process or cut up until coarsely chopped. Add tomatoes and process or chop just until combined; the mixture should be coarse. Set aside for at least 1 hour to allow flavors to blend. Taste for seasoning. Chill. Drain off excess liquid before serving.

Makes about 2½ cups

CORIANDER SPICE CAKE

This is a moist, gingerbread-like cake that keeps very well and actually improves in flavor the second or third day—if it lasts that long. A good way to use your coriander seed harvest.

2½ cups sifted all-purpose flour
2 teaspoons baking soda
1 teaspoon salt
2 teaspoons ground ginger
1 teaspoon ground cloves
1 teaspoon cinnamon
1 teaspoon ground coriander
** seed**
½ cup sugar
½ cup butter, melted
1 cup light molasses
2 eggs, slightly beaten
½ cup raisins
½ cup chopped walnuts
⅓ cup chopped candied orange
** peel**
1 cup boiling water

ORANGE BUTTER ICING

1 pound sifted powdered sugar
¼ teaspoon salt
½ cup butter, at room
** temperature**
3 to 4 tablespoons orange juice
2 teaspoons grated orange zest
** (orange part of the peel)**

Sift powdered sugar into mixing bowl, add salt and mix. Beat in the butter and add the orange juice a tablespoon at a time until you reach the desired consistency. Add orange zest and frost cooled cake.

Makes about 2 cups

Preheat oven to 350°F.

Grease a 9 × 13-inch baking pan. Sift flour, baking soda, salt and all the spices together. In a bowl, blend sugar with melted butter. Beat in molasses and eggs. Stir in raisins, walnuts and orange peel. Add sifted dry ingredients and hot water alternately to egg mixture, beating after each addition until just combined. Don't overmix. Pour into baking pan and bake for 30 minutes or until a cake tester inserted in center comes out clean. Sprinkle with confectioners' sugar or top with our Orange Butter icing (recipe at right).

Serves 16 to 18

HOMEMADE DILLED MUSTARD

The sweet and pungent homemade mustard is delicious with cold cuts, grilled sausages or cheese.

1 cup dry mustard
2 teaspoons salt
1 cup cider vinegar
¾ cup sugar
2 tablespoons finely chopped
**   fresh dill**
¼ cup water
2 eggs, slightly beaten

Mix all of the ingredients except the eggs. Cover and let stand several hours. Pour into the top of a double boiler and heat gently. Add the eggs, stirring constantly. Cook over simmering water 10 minutes until thickened. Pour into containers, cover and chill. Keep refrigerated.

Makes about 2 cups

DILLED SUMMER VEGETABLES

A particularly fine combination of flavors and colors. Perfect on a summer's day when you have a big harvest of these vegetables.

Steam together equal parts of fresh cut green beans, carrot chunks and summer squash cut into chunks. Season the hot, tender vegetables with salt, freshly ground pepper and butter to taste, then sprinkle very liberally with lots of finely chopped fresh dill. Mix and serve.

ROSY DILLED RADISH DIP

A rosy-pink all-purpose dip.

8 ounces cream cheese, at
**   room temperature**
1 tablespoon lemon juice
1 tablespoon chopped fresh dill
**   or 1 teaspoon dried**
1 clove garlic, minced
1 cup finely chopped radishes

GARNISH:
nasturtium or calendula
**   blossoms, or more sliced**
**   radishes**

Combine all ingredients well. Refrigerate for several hours before serving with crackers, chips or vegetable strips. Garnish with nasturtium or calendula flowers, or sliced radishes.

Makes about 2 cups

Lemon Thyme- or Basil-Stuffed Chicken Breasts

A light, creamy and savory summer dinner treat. The perfume of the fresh herbs combines beautifully with the chicken and "light" cream cheese.

6 half chicken breasts, skinned and boned
4 ounces "light" cream cheese
4 to 5 scallions, finely chopped
14 to 16 fresh basil leaves or 2 tablespoons lemon thyme leaves
½ teaspoon salt
½ teaspoon freshly ground pepper
1 teaspoon paprika
⅓ cup all-purpose flour
2 eggs, beaten with 2 teaspoons water
½ cup dried bread crumbs
½ cup freshly grated Parmesan or Swiss cheese
2 tablespoons melted butter or oil

Preheat oven to 350°F.

Place each chicken breast in a plastic bag or between sheets of waxed paper and pound with the edge of a mug or wooden mallet until just ⅛ inch thick. Roll each breast with a rolling pin to even and flatten. Spread 1 rounded tablespoon of the cream cheese down the center of each chicken piece. Sprinkle some of the chopped scallions and arrange basil leaves over the top of each flattened breast. If using lemon thyme, sprinkle 1 teaspoon of leaves over the cream cheese on each breast. Roll up jelly-roll fashion, tucking sides under. In a shallow pan, combine the salt, pepper, paprika and flour. Pour the eggs beaten with water into a second pan. In a third shallow pan, combine the crumbs and the grated cheese. Dip the rolled-up breasts first in the flour mixture, then the beaten eggs, and finish with a good coating of the crumb mixture. Place chicken on a greased baking sheet in a single layer and drizzle the melted butter over the tops of the breasts. Bake 20 to 25 minutes and serve immediately.

Serves 6

Lemon Thyme Bread

A light-textured teabread—great for the office or after-school snacks. Keeps well and elegantly satisfies afternoon cravings.

2 cups unbleached all-purpose flour
2 teaspoons baking powder
¼ teaspoon salt
6 tablespoons butter or margarine, at room temperature
1 cup sugar
2 eggs
1 tablespoon grated lemon zest (yellow part of peel)
2 tablespoon lemon juice
2 tablespoons finely chopped lemon thyme
⅔ cup milk

LEMON GLAZE:
2 tablespoons lemon juice mixed with enough powdered sugar (about ½ cup) to make a thin, pourable consistency

Preheat oven to 325°F.

Grease and flour an 8 × 4½-inch loaf pan. On a sheet of waxed paper, sift together flour, baking powder and salt. In a bowl, cream butter; gradually add sugar, beating until fluffy. Add eggs one at a time, beating well after each addition. Mix in lemon zest, lemon juice and lemon thyme. Add dry ingredients alternately with milk, mixing just until batter is smooth and blended. Pour batter into pan. Bake for 55 to 60 minutes or until a wooden pick inserted in the center of bread comes out clean. Let stand in pan for 5 minutes. Turn out and slowly pour lemon glaze over the loaf.

Makes 1 loaf

Fresh Apple Cake with Lemon Thyme

A good apple cake elevated to something special with the addition of the lemon thyme. Tastes good the first day and mellows beautifully if made ahead.

2 large tart apples, unpeeled, cut into ½-inch cubes—about 2½ cups
2½ tablespoons finely chopped lemon thyme leaves
1 tablespoon lemon juice
1 cup sugar
1½ cups all-purpose flour
1 teaspoon baking powder
½ teaspoon baking soda
¼ teaspoon salt
optional: ½ cup chopped nuts
2 eggs, lightly beaten
6 tablespoons butter, melted and cooled
1 teaspoon vanilla

Preheat oven to 350°F.

Grease and flour and 8 × 8 × 2-inch baking pan. Combine apples, lemon thyme, lemon juice and ½ cup of the sugar in a bowl and set aside. On a sheet of waxed paper or in a bowl, sift together flour, baking powder, soda and salt. Add remaining ½ cup sugar and nuts if used. Set aside. In a large bowl, beat eggs with melted butter and vanilla. Add apple-lemon thyme mixture, mixing until blended. Add dry ingredients, stirring until just combined. Spoon batter into prepared pan and bake 35 minutes or until cake tester comes out clean. Allow to cool and serve.

Serves 8 to 10

GRILLED CHICKEN WITH MINTY YOGURT SAUCE

A cool but tangy adaptation of a classic Indian dish.

**6 boned half chicken breasts
salt and freshly ground pepper
to taste**

**YOGURT SAUCE:
1 cup plain yogurt (lowfat okay)
3 cloves garlic, minced
1 teaspoon freshly grated ginger
1 tablespoon lime juice
⅔ cup chopped fresh mint leaves**

**GARNISH:
2 limes, sliced**

Sprinkle the chicken with salt and pepper. Place in a glass or non-aluminum dish and set aside.

Combine the yogurt, garlic, ginger, lime juice and mint leaves. Spoon over the chicken breasts, coating them thoroughly. Marinate overnight in the refrigerator.

Preheat the broiler (or prepare a charcoal grill). Grease the broiler pan and warm it about four inches from the heat. Using a slotted spoon, transfer the chicken to the heated pan, reserving the sauce.

Broil or grill the chicken until just tender, about ten minutes per side, turning the chicken skin side up during the last few minutes of cooking. Pour off the fat. Cover each breast with some of the reserved sauce and place back under the broiler to heat through. (If using the grill, warm the sauce through separately in a saucepan over gentle heat.) Transfer to a serving platter and garnish with the limes (and a few sprigs of mint, if you wish).

Serves 6

MINTED MELON

Mint and melon go together beautifully, as both these recipes prove.

**1 orange-fleshed melon, peeled, seeded and cut into large cubes
1 teaspoon grated orange rind
¼ cup orange juice
2 tablespoons sugar
⅓ cup raspberry vinegar
¼ cup finely chopped fresh mint**

Put melon in an attractive serving bowl. Mix other ingredients together well to dissolve sugar. Pour over melon. Chill covered for an hour to blend flavors.

Serves 4

MELON BRÛLÉE

Equally delightful over pound cake or solo.

**1 small honeydew melon, peeled, seeded and cut into chunks
1 small cantaloupe, peeled, seeded and cut into chunks
1 tablespoon sugar
2 teaspoons grated orange zest (orange part of peel)
½ cup orange juice
1 cup "light" sour cream
¾ cup firmly packed light brown sugar
2 tablespoons finely chopped mint**

Place melon evenly in a 1-quart oven-proof dish. Toss with sugar, orange zest and juice and set aside at room temperature for 1 to 2 hours.

Preheat broiler. Spread sour cream over melon and sprinkle with brown sugar. Place dish about 5 inches from the heat and broil for 2 to 3 minutes. Do not burn! Scatter mint on top and serve immediately.

Serves 4 to 6

Fresh Herb and Cheese Popovers

Who could resist these light and savory puffs? Great for brunch or Sunday breakfast.

2 eggs
1 cup all-purpose flour
¼ teaspoon freshly ground pepper
¼ teaspoon salt
1 cup milk
1 tablespoon vegetable oil
1 tablespoon chopped fresh oregano
½ cup chopped fresh basil
½ cup freshly grated Parmesan or Asiago cheese
2 tablespoons butter, softened for greasing

Preheat oven to 425°F.

Beat eggs in a large bowl. Add flour, pepper and salt, beating until slightly mixed. Gradually beat in the milk until the mixture is blended and smooth. Stir in oil, herbs and cheese.

Thoroughly grease 6 to 8 oven-proof custard cups (about 5-ounce size). Place cups on a baking sheet and warm in the oven for 2 to 3 minutes until the butter melts. Remove from oven and fill the cups half full with batter. Bake for 25 to 30 minutes, until golden. Don't peek in the oven while they're cooking or they'll collapse.

If you like your popovers especially crisp, taken them out of the oven when they're done, prick them with a skewer, loosen them in the cup and sit them at an angle. Turn off the oven, return the popovers, leaving door ajar, and let them sit in there for another 5 to 10 minutes.

Makes 6 to 8

Clams Coquilles Oregano

An unusual and savory appetizer.

2 tablespoons olive oil
1 onion, minced
2 small cloves garlic, minced
2 eight-ounce cans minced clams, drained and juice reserved
1 tablespoon finely chopped fresh parsley
2 teaspoons finely chopped fresh oregano
½ cup bread crumbs
⅛ teaspoon freshly ground pepper
6 slices bread, toasted and quartered
olive oil

TOPPING:
2 tablespoons bread crumbs
2 tablespoons freshly grated Parmesan cheese

Preheat oven to 375°F.

Mix together topping ingredients and set aside. In a small skillet, heat oil, add onions and garlic and sauté until softened. Remove from heat. Add clams, herbs, crumbs and pepper. Add enough of the reserved clam juice to moisten.

Place a spoonful on toast squares. Arrange on a baking sheet. Sprinkle with topping mixture, then sprinkle with a few drops of olive oil. Bake 10 minutes, then place under broiler for several minutes to lightly brown.

May be prepared one day ahead or frozen up to the point of baking.

Makes 24

Parsley Antipasto Salad

A mouthwatering and sprightly first-course salad, bright with color and flavor.

1 clove garlic, mashed to a paste
3 tablespoons fresh lemon juice
¼ cup olive oil
salt and pepper to taste
¼ cup Swiss cheese, cut into
  very small cubes
½ cup pecan meats, chopped
½ cup Italian broadleaf parsley,
  finely chopped
¼ cup quartered olives
¼ cup chopped red or yellow
  bell pepper
1 scallion, finely chopped
optional: ¼ cup finely
  chopped sun-dried tomatoes
  (see recipe p. 100)
large lettuce leaves for 4 salad
  plates

GARNISH:
parsley sprigs
lemon slices

Combine the garlic and lemon juice and add the oil in a stream, whisking the dressing until it is blended. Add salt and pepper to taste. Stir in the cheese, pecans, parsley, olives, chopped pepper, scallion and dried tomatoes, if used. Garnish and serve on lettuce-lined plates.

Serves 4

Gremolata

A traditional Italian condiment, we love it as a quick and healthy topping for lightly buttered baked potatoes, plain broiled chicken, or any mild-flavored baked fish or veal dish.

⅔ cup finely chopped fresh
  parsley
2 cloves garlic, minced
1½ tablespoons grated lemon
  zest (yellow part of peel)

Combine and mix all ingredients together thoroughly. Best if made at least 30 minutes in advance to allow flavors to blend.

Makes ⅔ cup

Linguini with Fresh Parsley Clam Sauce

A smooth, creamy and delicious quick sauce; parsley and clams just seem to go together.

2 small cloves garlic, minced
2 to 3 scallions, finely chopped
1 to 2 tablespoons olive oil
2 six-ounce cans chopped clams
1 cup half-and-half (or use whole milk)
1 cup finely chopped fresh parsley
1 cup freshly grated Parmesan or Asiago cheese
salt and pepper to taste
8 ounces linguini noodles

GARNISH:
1 large tomato, seeded, drained and coarsely chopped
juice of ½ lemon

Sauté garlic and scallions in olive oil until soft. Add clam juice from canned clams and the half-and-half and simmer until reduced and thickened, 8 to 10 minutes. Stir in clams and parsley and simmer another 5 minutes. Add cheese, stir, and add salt and pepper to taste. Cook the linguini in boiling, salted water and drain. Heat sauce through and mix with hot linguine. Garnish with chopped tomato and sprinkle lemon juice over the top. Serve immediately, piping hot.

Serves 4 to 6

Garbanzo Bean and Parsley Dip

The addition of fresh parsley freshens and finishes the nutty, mild beans in this version of a '60s standard we all enjoy often.

1¾ cups cooked or 1 fifteen-ounce can garbanzo beans, drained and liquid reserved
1 clove garlic, minced
3 tablespoons lemon juice
⅓ cup tahini (sesame seed paste)
2 scallions, chopped
½ teaspoon ground cumin
¼ teaspoon soy sauce
½ cup chopped parsley
salt and pepper to taste
pinch of cayenne

GARNISH:
chopped fresh mint and/or parsley leaves

In a food processor or blender, combine beans, ¼ cup of the bean liquid, garlic, lemon juice, tahini, scallions, cumin, soy sauce and parsley. Process until mixture is smooth. (If mixture seems too thick, add a little extra garbanzo bean liquid.) Taste for seasoning, adding salt, pepper and cayenne. Add fresh herb garnishes.

Serve with pita bread triangles or crispy crackers.

Serves 6 to 8

Noisettes d'Agneau Persillade
Parsleyed Lamb Chops

This dish is classic, elegant and easily prepared. It is especially good made with fresh single-leaf parsley.

PERSILLADE TOPPING:
½ cup bread crumbs
6 tablespoons fresh parsley, minced
2 tablespoons minced scallions or shallots
1 clove garlic, minced
3 tablespoons melted butter or margarine
1 teaspoon grated lemon zest (yellow part of peel)

8 lamb chops, 1½ inches thick
salt and pepper to taste
3 tablespoons butter
3 tablespoons finely chopped shallots or scallions
⅓ cup dry white wine or dry vermouth

GARNISH:
lemon slices

Prepare persillade topping: Combine bread crumbs, parsley, shallots, garlic, melted butter and lemon rind. Set aside.

Carefully remove the bones from lamb chops. Leave all but a thin layer of fat on. Sprinkle with salt and pepper. Melt butter in a large heavy skillet. Stir in the shallots and sauté lightly. Add lamb chops and brown on all sides, then cook about 5 to 8 minutes, or longer depending on the doneness desired. Remove lamb chops to a baking dish.

Spoon off excess fat from skillet. Add wine and cook, scraping up all particles in bottom of pan. Simmer 3 to 4 minutes until wine is reduced to half. Pour mixture over lamb. Spread a portion of the persillade topping on each chop, pressing it down slightly. (May be prepared ahead to this point.)

Bake 5 minutes at 350°F or until heated through. Garnish with lemon slices and serve.

Serves 4

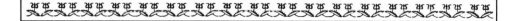

Rosemary-Basil Chicken Wings

For hors d'oeuvres or a tasty light meal. We find these spicy tidbits are delicious eaten cold the next day, too, so make a double recipe!

MARINADE:
1 lemon
2 cloves garlic, minced
2 tablespoons butter
2 tablespoons olive oil
3 tablespoons white wine
½ teaspoon freshly ground
  pepper
1 teaspoon fresh rosemary,
  crumbled, or ½ teaspoon dried
¼ cup chopped fresh basil
½ teaspoon salt

2 pounds chicken wings (about
  24), prepared as "drummettes"
  if available. Otherwise cut off
  wing tips and cut wings at the
  joint to create 2 winglets.

GARNISH:
fresh basil sprigs

Grate 1 tablespoon lemon zest and put into a small heavy saucepan. Squeeze the juice from the lemon into the pan. Add remaining marinade ingredients, heat, and then simmer for 5 minutes. Pour marinade over chicken wings and toss. Marinate at least ½ hour to blend flavors.

Preheat oven to 425°F. Bake the chicken wings on a baking sheet in the preheated oven for 20 to 25 minutes until glazed and browned. Garnish with fresh basil sprigs. Can also be barbecued over moderately hot coals. Serve warm or cold.

Serves 6 to 8

Glazed Fruited Chicken with Rosemary

The aromatic, piney scent of rosemary sets off the glazed dried fruits beautifully in this very satisfying main dish.

4 half chicken breasts
4 chicken thighs
salt and pepper or seasoned salt
1 clove garlic, minced

SAUCE:
1 cup water
1 cup dry white wine
2 tablespoons lemon juice
¼ cup honey
2 teaspoons hot dry mustard
2 teaspoons finely chopped fresh
  rosemary, or 1 teaspoon dried
½ cup pitted prunes
½ cup dried apricots
1 large fresh apple, cored and
  sliced into rings

GARNISH:
chopped parsley

Preheat over to 350°F.

Halve the chicken portions and sprinkle with salt and pepper. Rub with garlic. Place on a 9 × 13-inch baking pan, skin side up. Bake 45 minutes. Meanwhile, prepare sauce.

In a saucepan, combine water, wine, lemon juice, honey, mustard and rosemary. Bring mixture to a boil and simmer 15 minutes. Add prunes, apricots and apple slices and simmer another 15 minutes or until liquid is reduced by half and fruit is tender. Remove chicken from oven. Pour off fat and skin chicken if desired. Spoon fruit sauce over chicken. Turn oven temperature up to 400°F. Return chicken to oven and bake for 15 minutes longer, basting once or twice. Sprinkle with chopped parsley. Serve hot with noodles or rice.

Serves 6

HERBED FRESH MUSHROOM PÂTÉ

This fine appetizer has a rich taste and meaty texture.

**1 pound fresh mushrooms
2 tablespoons butter
½ cup finely chopped onion
½ teaspoon salt
2 teaspoons finely chopped
    fresh thyme
⅛ teaspoon freshly ground
    pepper
1 tablespoon brandy
2 hard-boiled eggs
1 teaspoon lemon juice
2 tablespoons mayonnaise
2 tablespoons finely chopped
    parsley
crackers or melba toast**

Rinse, pat dry and finely chop mushrooms, or coarsely grate in food processor. In a large skillet, melt butter. Add mushrooms, onion, salt, thyme and pepper. Cook over moderate heat, stirring often, until all liquid has evaporated, about 10 minutes. Add brandy. Cook, stirring constantly, until brandy evaporates, about 1 minute. Cool. Reserve 1 egg yolk. Finely chop remaining 1 whole egg and 1 egg white. Add to mushroom mixture with lemon juice, mayonnaise and parsley. Mix well. Turn into a 1½-cup container. Cover and chill. At serving time, pack into small serving dish and unmold onto lettuce on a serving plate. Using a small fine mesh sieve held directly over serving bowl, sieve reserved egg yolk over top. Serve with crackers or melba toast.

Serves 8 to 10

GORGONZOLA AND FRESH THYME SAUCE FOR PASTA

**1½ cups half-and-half
6 ounces top quality aged
    Gorgonzola cheese, crumbled
1 teaspoon fresh thyme
3 to 4 generous grates fresh
    nutmeg or ⅛ teaspoon ground
    white pepper to taste**

Combine half-and-half, crumbled Gorgonzola, fresh thyme and nutmeg. Cook gently, stirring frequently, until mixture reduces by one-fourth. Add white pepper to taste. Toss with steaming pasta.

You may add sliced, peeled apples and walnuts to the above. Offer extra nutmeg.

Serves 2 to 3

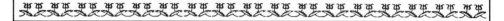

EDIBLE FLOWERS

BLOSSOM TEA SANDWICHES

Open-faced finger sandwiches that offer a handsome smorgasbord of colors and flavors. Decorate each sandwich with several savory edible flower petals and herb blossoms and serve. Expect to be applauded for your artistry!

1 large cucumber, peeled, seeded
  and finely chopped
8 ounces cream cheese ("light"
  style okay), at room temperature
¾ teaspoon Worcestershire sauce
¼ teaspoon minced garlic
1 teaspoon salt
¼ cup finely chopped chives
  or scallions
thinly sliced cracked wheat or
  white bread, crusts removed
lots of edible blossoms:
  nasturtium blossoms, chive
  blossoms, borage flowers,
  calendula petals, pea or bean
  flowers, herb blossoms, rinsed
  and patted dry

Squeeze chopped cucumber in a kitchen towel to remove as much moisture as possible; set aside. Blend together the cream cheese, seasonings and chives or scallion. Add cucumber and combine well but do not overmix. Spread on bread and cut into finger-sized open sandwiches. To serve: decorate the tops of the sandwiches with petals of various edible flowers, combining colors and shapes to suit your palate and your fancy.

Anise Hyssop

Marinated Anise Hyssop Baked Chicken

The flavors of ginger and anise hyssop add a fine perfume to this sumptuous main dish.

> 1 frying chicken (2½ to 3½ pounds), jointed
>
> MARINADE:
> 1 tablespoon chopped fresh ginger
> 1 cup finely chopped anise hyssop leaves and flowers
> 1 teaspoon cinnamon
> 3 cloves garlic, minced
> 3 tablespoons oil
> 3 tablespoons soy sauce

Mix marinade ingredients together and spread evenly over the chicken pieces right in the baking pan. Marinate for 2 to 4 hours.

Preheat oven to 375°F.

Bake for 45 minutes to an hour or until chicken is cooked and browned. Serve with fluffy rice.

Serves 3 to 4

Berries Served with Anise Hyssop Cream

Rinse, drain and chill 1 box of blueberries or raspberries. Blend a little honey to taste with ½ cup of yogurt, sour cream or slightly whipped cream and 1 tablespoon minced anise hyssop. Spoon sauce over berries and garnish with anise hyssop flowers.

Serves 2

Anise Hyssop Tea

Harvest long sprigs of anise hyssop leaves. Rinse, shake off excess water and hang to dry in a cool, dark place (or dry in a dehydrator). Pour boiling water over sprigs and let steep.

This makes a naturally sweet-flavored and refreshing hot or iced tea with a licorice flavor.

SPECIAL TREASURE CHINESE BEEF WITH ANISE HYSSOP

The anise hyssop adds a subtle flavor that enhances all the other ingredients in this simple and delicious dish. Serve with fluffy white rice.

> 1 pound flank steak, cut across the grain into strips 3 inches long and ½ inch wide
> ½ cup chopped anise hyssop flowers and leaves
> ⅓ cup soy sauce
> 1 tablespoon brown sugar
> 2 tablespoons sherry
> 2 tablespoons vegetable oil
> ¼ cup chicken stock
> 2 teaspoons cornstarch, dissolved in 2 teaspoons water

Combine flank steak with chopped anise hyssop, soy sauce, brown sugar and sherry. Marinate several hours.

Remove meat from marinade, reserving any remaining sauce. Heat wok or large skillet, add oil and stir-fry meat quickly over medium-high heat until brown. Add chicken stock and remaining marinade and heat through. Stir in cornstarch mixture and cook, stirring until thickened.

Serves 4 to 6

LEMONY ANISE HYSSOP TEA BREAD

The delicate flavors of anise and lemon will please those who do not like things too sweet.

> 2 cups all-purpose flour
> 1 tablespoon baking powder
> ½ teaspoon salt
> ½ cup butter, at room temperature
> ½ cup sugar
> grated zest of one lemon (yellow part of peel)
> ⅓ to ½ cup anise hyssop flowers, finely chopped
> 2 eggs, beaten
> ½ cup lemon juice
> ½ cup chopped walnuts

Preheat oven to 350°F. Grease and flour an 8½ × 4½-inch bread or loaf pan.

Stir together flour, baking powder and salt in a bowl. In another bowl, cream butter with sugar until fluffy, then add lemon zest, chopped flowers and the beaten eggs, and beat mixture just until thoroughly combined. Stir in the lemon juice. Gradually mix in the dry ingredients and nuts, mixing until blended. Spoon into prepared pan and bake 50 to 55 minutes. Cool on rack. Best-tasting when wrapped in foil and sliced the next day. Keeps well.

Makes 1 loaf

Anise Hyssop Carrots

1 to 2 tablespoons butter
2 tablespoons water
1 pound carrots, very thinly
    sliced
3 tablespoons fresh anise
    hyssop, very finely chopped
1 tablespoon lemon juice
optional: salt to taste

In a saucepan, melt butter, add water, and steam carrots, chopped anise hyssop and lemon juice for 6 to 10 minutes, just until tender but still crisp. Salt to taste. Serve immediately.

Serves 4 to 6

Anise Hyssop Honey Butter

½ cup honey
¾ cup butter, at room
    temperature
2 tablespoons chopped anise
    hyssop flowers

Combine honey and butter, mixing until well creamed. Blend in flowers.
   Serve in a crock to use on pancakes, waffles or muffins. Store in refrigerator.

Makes about 1 cup

Anise Hyssop Flower Drop Cookies

1 bunch anise hyssop flowers
3 eggs
1 cup sugar
½ teaspoon vanilla
2 cups all-purpose flour
1 teaspoon baking powder
½ teaspoon salt

Preheat oven to 325°. Line 2 to 3 cookie sheets with aluminum foil; lightly grease.
   Strip petals of anise hyssop flowers to measure ⅓ cup. Chop fine. With an electric mixer, beat eggs until thick and lemon colored. Add sugar and flower petals and beat for 5 minutes. Add vanilla.
   Sift together flour, baking powder and salt and add to egg mixture. Continue beating for 5 minutes longer. Drop batter by teaspoonfuls onto lined cookie sheets, spacing well apart. Bake until they begin to color, about 12 to 15 minutes.

Makes about 3 dozen

BORAGE

BORAGE AND CUCUMBERS IN SOUR CREAM DRESSING

3 long cucumbers
salt
1 cup sour cream or fresh
  plain yogurt
2 tablespoons rice vinegar
½ teaspoon celery seed
¼ cup chopped scallions
1 teaspoon sugar
¼ cup finely chopped very
  young borage leaves
salt and freshly ground pepper
  to taste

GARNISH:
borage flowers or chive blossoms

Wash, score and very thinly slice the cucumbers. Salt lightly and let stand in a colander for 30 minutes to drain. Rinse off the salt and pat dry with paper towels.

In a bowl, mix remaining ingredients, adding salt and pepper to taste. Add cucumbers and toss lightly. Garnish with borage flowers or chive blossoms. Refrigerate 1 hour before serving.

Serves 6 to 8

VICHYSSOISE WITH BORAGE FLOWERS

6 large leeks, white parts only
¼ cup butter
4 cups chicken stock
3 medium potatoes, peeled
  and diced
2 tablespoons chopped very
  young borage leaves
1 cup sour cream (or ½ cup plain
  yogurt and ½ cup sour cream)
salt and white pepper to taste
dash nutmeg

GARNISH:
borage flowers
3 tablespoons chopped chives

Slice the leeks into thin slivers. Melt butter in a large saucepan; add leeks and sauté over moderate heat until softened. Add chicken stock, potatoes and borage leaves. Bring to a boil and simmer covered for 35 minutes or until potatoes are tender. Strain the stock. Purée the vegetables in a food processor or blender. Combine stock and purée. Chill overnight.

Just before serving, stir in 1 cup sour cream. Add salt, pepper and a dash of nutmeg. Serve in chilled soup bowls; garnish with borage flowers and chopped chives.

Serves 6

Borage Garnishes

Lavender-blue borage blossoms make attractive edible garnishes. Try them on grapefruit halves or orange sections and in any fruit salad; in potato or green salad or with sliced hard-boiled eggs or cold poached salmon. Use them as decorations on frosted cakes or frozen in ice cubes and added to herb teas.

Borage Tea

A very traditional herb tea.

In a warmed teapot put ½ cup finely chopped borage leaves and flowers. Pour in two cups of freshly made boiling water. Cover and let steep for 5 to 6 minutes. Strain and serve hot with honey and lemon as desired.

Borage tea is also refreshing as an iced tea; make it stronger and serve over ice cubes that have blue borage flowers frozen in their centers for an especially cooling drink.

Serves 2

Calendulas

Orange-Calendula Drop Cookies

6 to 8 fresh calendula blossoms
½ cup butter, at room temperature
½ cup white sugar
grated zest of 2 oranges (orange part of peel)
2 tablespoons orange juice concentrate, at room temperature
1 teaspoon vanilla
2 eggs, lightly beaten
2 cups all-purpose flour
2½ teaspoons baking powder
¼ teaspoon salt
1 cup almond halves

Preheat oven to 350°F. Lightly grease 2 cookie sheets.

Rinse calendulas. Pull off petals and set aside. In a bowl, cream butter, sugar and orange rind until fluffy. Add orange juice concentrate and vanilla. Mix in eggs, stirring until blended.

Sift together flour, baking powder and salt. Blend calendula petals and dry ingredients into creamed mixture. Drop dough by teaspoonfuls onto cookie sheet. Press an almond half into each cookie. Bake 12 to 15 minutes until golden brown.

Makes 3 to 4 dozen

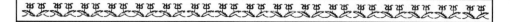

Calendula Confetti Eggs
Scrambled Eggs with Calendula Petals

8 eggs
6 tablespoons milk
pinch of nutmeg
salt and pepper to taste
2 tablespoons butter
petals only from five large
  calendula flowers, coarsely
  chopped
4 slices toast or 4 muffins,
  buttered
optional topping: several
  tablespoons grated cheese

Beat the eggs with the milk and seasonings. Melt the butter in a skillet and scramble the eggs. Just before eggs are done, stir in the chopped petals. Pile the eggs on top of buttered toast or muffins and serve right away, topping with cheese if desired.

Serves 4

Tangerine Cole Slaw with Calendula Flower Garnish

2 cups unpeeled, chopped red
  apple
2 tablespoons freshly grated
  tangerine peel
3 cups fresh tangerine
  segments, seeded*
2 tablespoons chopped green
  bell pepper
5 cups finely shredded cabbage
12 calendula flowers

DRESSING:
⅓ cup sour cream
¼ cup mayonnaise
1 tablespoon lemon juice
1 tablespoon vinegar
2 tablespoons honey
½ teaspoon each mustard and
  celery seed
½ teaspoon salt
⅛ teaspoon freshly ground
  pepper

GARNISH:
calendula blossoms

Combine apple, tangerine peel, tangerine segments and chopped green pepper with cabbage in a large bowl. Remove calendula petals from flowers and add the petals to the salad.

Blend together dressing ingredients and pour over cole slaw. Toss lightly to mix well. Taste for additional seasoning. Chill thoroughly. Garnish with whole yellow and orange calendula blossoms.

Serves 6 to 8

*Canned, drained mandarin orange segments may also be used, with grated orange peel substituted for tangerine peel.

CREAMY CALENDULA SOUFFLÉ

This blender soufflé goes together quickly and has a fine color and flavor. Good both fresh from the oven and cut into squares the next day.

2 tablespoons soft butter
2 tablespoons grated
   Parmesan cheese
6 eggs
¼ cup grated Parmesan cheese
½ cup half-and-half
1 teaspoon prepared mustard
½ teaspoon salt
⅛ teaspoon cayenne pepper
dash of nutmeg
8 ounces sharp Cheddar cheese,
   cut into small pieces
10 ounces cream cheese, cut
   into small pieces
½ cup calendula petals

GARNISH:
calendula flowers

Preheat oven to 375°F.

Spread butter inside a 5-cup soufflé dish or other deep baking dish or 6 individual baking dishes. Sprinkle with the 2 tablespoons Parmesan cheese.

In a blender or food processor, place eggs, ¼ cup Parmesan cheese, half-and-half, mustard, salt, pepper and nutmeg. Process or whirl until smooth.

Add Cheddar cheese piece by piece while motor is running. Add cream cheese and process for 5 seconds. Stir in calendula petals. Pour soufflé mixture into prepared dish.

Bake for 45 to 50 minutes (bake individual soufflés 15 to 20 minutes). Tops should be golden brown and slightly cracked; don't overbake. Serve immediately, garnishing with whole calendula flowers.

Serves 5 to 6

CURRY RISOTTO WITH CALENDULA PETALS

6 tablespoons butter or margarine
1½ onions, finely chopped
2 teaspoons curry powder
1 cup rice
1 rounded tablespoon tomato
   paste
2 cups chicken stock
bouquet garni: 2 sprigs parsley,
   1 bay leaf, 2 sprigs fresh thyme
   or ½ teaspoon dried, can be
   tied in cheesecloth or placed
   in a metal tea infuser
½ cup calendula petals
salt and freshly ground pepper
   to taste

GARNISH:
1 cubed avocado
pimiento strips or diced red
   peppers
calendula petals

In a heavy-bottomed saucepan with lid, melt 4 tablespoons of the butter. Add onions and sauté until softened. Add curry powder and rice and stir over medium heat for 2 minutes. Add tomato paste, chicken stock and bouquet garni. Cover tightly and simmer until tender, about 20 minutes. Remove bouquet garni. Just before serving add remaining 2 tablespoons butter and the calendula petals. Season with salt and pepper to taste. Heat through and serve garnished with avocado cubes, pimiento or red pepper strips and a sprinkling of calendula petals.

Serves 6

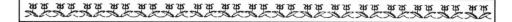

CALENDULA LEMON PUDDING CAKE

A tempting dessert with lovely lemon flavors.
Not at all rich, so you can indulge yourself!

¾ cup sugar
¼ cup unbleached all-purpose flour
⅛ teaspoon salt
2 tablespoons melted butter
1 tablespoon grated lemon zest
  (yellow part of peel)
5 tablespoons lemon juice
3 egg yolks
1½ cups milk
3 egg whites, at room temperature
⅛ teaspoon cream of tartar
¼ cup sugar
6 tablespoons calendula petals

GARNISH:
calendula petals
whipped cream

Preheat oven to 350°F. Lightly grease a 1½-quart baking dish or 6 custard cups. Set into a slightly larger pan, at least 2 inches deep.

In a mixing bowl, combine the ¾ cup sugar, flour and salt. Add butter, lemon zest and lemon juice and mix until thoroughly blended. With a whisk, beat egg yolks until thick and lemon colored; add milk and mix well. Combine with lemon mixture, stirring until blended.

In another bowl, beat egg whites until foamy, add cream of tartar and beat until soft peaks form. Add the ¼ cup of sugar gradually and beat until stiff but not dry. Fold the whites and calendula petals into lemon mixture. Spoon into baking dish or custard cups. Pour 1 inch of hot water around them.

Bake until set and top is golden brown, about 35 minutes for custard cups or 45 minutes for baking dish. Remove from water and let cool on a wire rack. Serve warm or chilled with a dollop of whipped cream and a sprinkle of additional calendula petals.

Serves 6

CHIVE BLOSSOMS

POTATO SALAD WITH CHIVE BLOSSOM MAYONNAISE

2 pounds small, thin-skinned
  boiling potatoes
⅓ cup white wine or rice
  vinegar
¼ teaspoon salt
pinch of pepper
¼ teaspoon dry mustard
¼ teaspoon sugar
1 tablespoon grated onion

DRESSING:
1 cup prepared mayonnaise
  (or use ½ cup mayonnaise
  and ½ cup fresh plain yogurt)
1 clove garlic, crushed
3 tablespoons chive blossom
  florets and chopped leaves
1 heaping teaspoon grated lemon
  zest (yellow part of peel)
2 teaspoons lemon juice
1 tablespoon each finely chopped
  parsley and green pepper
salt and pepper to taste

GARNISH:
whole chive blossoms

Boil or steam potatoes until tender
when pierced. Let cool slightly, then
peel and slice. Heat vinegar with salt,
pepper, mustard and sugar and
sprinkle over potatoes. Mix in grated
onion. Toss well and cool. Combine
the dressing ingredients. Mix with
potatoes. Add salt and pepper to
taste. Garnish with whole chive
blossoms and serve.

Serves 6 to 8

CHEESY CHIVE BLOSSOM OMELET

4 eggs
1 teaspoon water
¼ teaspoon salt, or to taste
⅛ teaspoon white pepper
1 teaspoon chopped fresh parsley
1 tablespoon unsalted butter
3 young chive blossoms, broken
  into individual florets
2 tablespoons grated Swiss cheese

GARNISH:
whole chive blossoms

In a small bowl, whisk together eggs,
water, salt, pepper and parsley. Melt
butter in a 10-inch omelet pan over
high heat until butter sizzles but has
not started to brown. Pour in egg
mixture, shaking pan immediately.
With the flat side of a fork stir eggs
and move and tilt pan in a circular
motion until eggs begin to set.
Sprinkle chive florets and cheese
down the center; allow cheese to melt
slightly, then fold omelet over and
serve. Garnish with blossoms.

Serves 2

CHIVE BLOSSOM VINEGAR

Fill a clean glass or plastic jar half full
of mature chive blossoms which have
not started to fade in color. Fill the
jar with white distilled vinegar or
rice vinegar (the mildest flavored),
making sure all the blossoms are
covered. Cap with a non-metal lid
and set in the sun. In about a week
the chive blossoms will have trans-
ferred their lovely color and flavor to
the liquid. Strain through cheesecloth
and dilute with more vinegar if you
find it too strong. Decant into any
attractive glass jars or bottles and seal
with corks or non-metal tops.

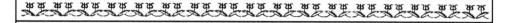

Johnny Jump-Ups

Johnny Jump-Up Flowers as Edible Garnishes

These dainty, pretty flowers have myriad uses. Here is a list of some of our favorite ways of enjoying them as "edible art."

— Set off a simple desert by combining fresh pineapple and kiwi slices with a small amount of kirsch and decorate with johnny jump-up blossoms. Also try this with bananas and oranges (or tangerines).

— Perk up everyday cottage cheese and fruit salads by garnishing with johnny jump-ups.

— For a romantic effect, decorate any frosted cake with fresh johnny jump-up flowers.

— Surround scoops of orange, pineapple or lemon sherbet with johnny jump-up flowers and mint leaves.

— Circle any pale-colored dip or spread, e.g., avocado, cream cheese, tuna, etc., with johnny jump-up flowers.

— Garnish plates of smoked or poached salmon with johnny jump-up flowers to set off its rosy color.

— Marinated vegetable salads, deviled eggs, and potato salads look appetizing when garnished with johnny jump-ups.

— Any green salad will be appetizing with an additional garnish of johnny jump-ups. Add them along with some mandarin slices for a particularly delicious effect.

Grapefruit Cups Cassis

This recipe is as attractive as it is appetizing and is especially nice for brunch. To whet appetites, have the grapefruits on the table when everyone sits down.

4 grapefruits
2 oranges, sectioned
⅔ cup crème de cassis or any good fruit liqueur
1 cup strawberries, sliced

GARNISH:
johnny jump-up flowers
mint leaves

In a sawtooth fashion, cut the grapefruits in half. Carefully section out the fruit, reserving shells for serving. Cut out and discard white membrane. Peel oranges, removing membrane; cut into sections. Place grapefruit and orange sections in a bowl, pouring off excess juice. Pour crème de cassis (or other fruit liqueur) over fruit and chill for at least one hour.

At serving time, add berries to grapefruit and oranges. Spoon fruit mixture into reserved grapefruit shells or glass bowls. Garnish with johnny jump-ups and sprigs of mint.

Serves 8

HERB AND FLOWER CHEESE TERRINE

Lovely and special party fare. Decorate the top and sides of the terrine with extra flowers, then serve it in slices to show off the layered effect.

1 pound very soft cream cheese
¾ cup very soft unsalted butter,
  at room temperature
1 cup grated Asiago or very fresh
  Parmesan cheese
2 large cloves garlic, minced
¾ cup finely chopped fresh basil
¼ cup finely chopped fresh oregano
2 teaspoons Worcestershire sauce
¾ teaspoon white pepper
¾ cup toasted pine nuts or pecans
¾ cup finely chopped fresh
  parsley
salt to taste
1¾ to 2 pounds Italian Provolone
  cheese, thinly sliced
25 to 30 johnny jump-up flowers,
  more if you have them, and
  additional edible flowers
  if available

Cream together the softened cream cheese, butter and Asiago or Parmesan cheese. Add the garlic, basil, oregano, Worcestershire sauce and white pepper and combine thoroughly. Add the pine nuts and chopped parsley and mix again (we suggest using your hands and "squooshing" it together). Salt mixture to taste, if desired.

Butter a bread or terrine pan. Line with waxed paper or parchment paper. Layer bottom of pan with Provolone cheese slices, then add a layer of the soft cheese mixture and a sprinkling of the johnny jump-up flowers. Continue to alternate layers of Provolone, soft cheese mixture and flowers. Try to get about 5 layers for a nice effect.

Refrigerate overnight. Remove from refrigerator and let stand about 15 minutes before turning out onto a serving platter. Remove paper and garnish with more johnny jump-ups (and other additional edible flowers if available). Serve in slices.

Serves 15 to 20

NASTURTIUMS

CENTERFOLD NASTURTIUM SALAD

Both the leaves and blossoms have a fine watercress-like flavor.

Arrange 15 rinsed nasturtium leaves around the outside edges of a large, flat plate. Lay 15 clean nasturtium flowers on top of the leaves, with their stems pointing to the center of the dish.

Working toward the center of the plate, next add a layer of very finely sliced sweet onions, then a layer of three very thinly sliced tomatoes and a layer of 2 to 3 large stalks of celery, finely chopped. Continue the layers as above until the dish is full. Sprinkle ½ cup of vinaigrette dressing over the salad and garnish by sprinkling with a finely chopped hard-boiled egg. Borage flowers also make a nice garnish.

Cover the salad and refrigerate for several hours to let the nasturtiums and other flavors blend before serving.

Serves 4

NASTURTIUM SHRIMP APPETIZER SALAD

1 tablespoon fresh lime juice
¼ cup olive oil
salt and freshly ground pepper to taste
1 cup cooked, shelled shrimp, coarsely chopped
¼ cup finely chopped onion
1 small tomato, cubed
½ avocado, peeled and cubed
2 tablespoons chopped nasturtium leaves
2 tablespoons chopped fresh cilantro
¼ cup chopped fresh basil
lettuce leaves
nasturtium flowers

Place lime juice in a small bowl. Whisk in the oil and season to taste with salt and pepper. Add the shrimp and onion and toss lightly. Let stand for 15 minutes to let flavors blend.

Add in the tomato, avocado and chopped nasturtium leaves, cilantro, and basil. Mound on lettuce leaves and surround with fresh whole nasturtium flowers.

Serves 2 to 4

NASTURTIUM SANDWICH FILLINGS

Add chopped clean nasturtium flower petals to your favorite tuna, egg or chicken salad sandwich fillings. They will give them a colorful lift and tangy bit of flavor. Blend nasturtium petals with cream cheese or butter and spread on thin slices of dark bread for savory snacks or appetizers.

NASTURTIUM VINEGAR

Combine 12 rinsed and dried nasturtium flowers and 1 cup of white wine vinegar in a glass jar with a screw-on lid. (If the lid is metal, line it with plastic wrap.) Put on the lid and let the flowers steep for about 3 weeks to a month. Strain the jewel-colored vinegar through cheesecloth and rebottle in a pretty bottle. Use the vinegar with a fine oil for a delicious vinaigrette dressing.

Makes 1 cup

PICKLED NASTURTIUM SEEDS

Collect nasturtium seeds when they become small and green and soak them in brine to cover, made from 1 quart water mixed with ½ cup salt. Renew the brine every 3 days until enough seeds have been collected.

Drain the seeds and pack them in small jars. Pour over enough boiling white wine vinegar to cover, seal and store for about a week before using. Use as a piquant substitute for capers in any recipe.

BABY SQUASH, NASTURTIUM BLOSSOMS AND HERBS WITH PASTA

This herbed sauce is lovely on pasta with the bright colors of the petals and squashes.

18 to 20 nasturtium flowers
1 tablespoon chopped fresh thyme
1 tablespoon fresh sweet marjoram
¼ cup chopped Italian broadleaf parsley
4 scallions, very finely chopped
3 small cloves garlic, minced
¼ cup fresh basil, coarsely chopped
2 tablespoons unsalted butter, softened
salt and pepper to taste
6 baby yellow scallop squash with their blossoms
6 baby zucchini squash with their blossoms
½ cup chicken stock
squash blossoms
fettucine noodles for 2 people

Separate the nasturtium petals from their bases, discard bases and chop the petals coarsely. Blend together with chopped herbs, scallion, garlic and butter and season with salt and pepper to taste. Allow the herb butter to stand for a half hour to let the flavors blend together. Cut the squashes into thin slices and the blossoms into strips. In a skillet, melt 2 tablespoons of the herb butter and sauté the squash for 3 minutes. Add the chicken stock and squash blossoms and simmer over low heat for a few minutes. Heat salted water for the pasta and cook the pasta until done to your taste. Drain pasta well and add with the rest of the herb butter to the squash. Correct seasonings, mix well, garnish and serve immediately.

Serves 2

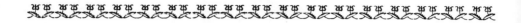

Some Other Uses for Herbs

Beef   garlic and regular chives, marjoram, oregano, savory, thyme

Breads   lemon basil, dill, marjoram, oregano, rosemary, thyme, lemon thyme

Cheese   basil, chervil, dill, fennel, garlic and regular chives, rosemary, thyme and lemon thyme

Eggs   basil, garlic and regular chives, oregano, parsley, tarragon

Fish   anise and lemon basil, chervil, dill, garlic and regular chives, parsley, tarragon, thyme and lemon thyme

Fruit   anise, cinnamon and lemon basils, ground coriander, lemon thyme, mint, rosemary

Lamb   arugula, garlic chives, lemon basil, lemon thyme, marjoram, mint, oregano, rosemary, savory, thyme *(make little slits and insert herbs before cooking)*

Pork   coriander/cilantro, garlic chives, lemon thyme, sage, thyme

Poultry   scented basils, regular and garlic chives, oregano, parsley, rosemary, sage, tarragon, thyme

Salads   basil, chervil, cilantro, dill, garlic and regular chives, marjoram, mint, parsley, sorrel *(all can also be made into herb vinegar for extra flavor)*

Soups   basil, dill, garlic and regular chives, lemon thyme, marjoram, mint, parsley, thyme

Vegetables basils, chervil, dill, garlic and regular chives, lemon thyme, marjoram, mint, oregano, parsley, rosemary, tarragon, thyme

INDEX

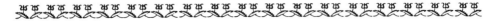

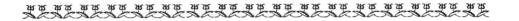

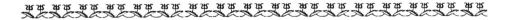

Fire and Ice Tomato Salad, 102
Fresh Tomato Corn Soup, 39
Fresh Tomato Sauce Santa Fe, 103
Green Tomato and Apple Chutney, 102
Homemade Creole Sauce with Chicken
    or Shrimp, 64
in Layered Greek Salad, 85
Pasta with Fresh Chile Pepper and
    Tomato Sauce, 98
Pasta with Fresh Tomatoes, Herbs and
    Garlic Sauce, 99
Pesto Stuffed, 108
in Roasted Garlic Dressing, 82
Salsa Cruda, 101
Sun-Dried Herb, 100
Tomato-Lemon Chutney, 98
Tomato, Opal Basil and Mozzarella
    Salad, 99
Tuscan Pizza, 103
Turnips, French Braised Carrots and, 22

V
Vegetables
    See also specific vegetables
    Baby, Hot Dipping Sauce for, 86
    Baby, Sorrel and Shallot Butter for, 86
    Dilled Summer, 125
    herbs used with, 149
    Poached Baby, Honey-Herb Dressing
        for, 86
Vegetarian main dishes
    See also Eggs; Pasta
    Baked Fresh Tomatoes, 101
    Baked Spinach Gnocchi, 88
    Corralitos Rice Casserole, 36
    Crustless Spinach Pie, 87
    Fresh Zucchini Rellenos, 95
    Marty's Basil-Rice Salad, 110

Mexican Fondue, 32
Stuffed Herbed Zucchini, 90
Tex-Mex Casserole, 33
Zucchini Pancakes, 96
Vinegars
    Chive Blossom, 145
    Scented Basil, 112

W
Watercress. *See* Cresses
Watermelon. *See* Melon
Winter squash. *See* Pumpkin

Y
Yellow peppers. *See* Bell peppers
Yellow squash
    Baby Squash, Nasturtium Blossoms and
        Herbs with Pasta, 148
    with Basil, Pepperoni and Parmesan, 90
    Blossoms, Ricotta-Stuffed, 94
    Gingered Peas and, 59
    Summer Squash Chowder, 93

Z
Zucchini
    Baby Squash, Nasturtium Blossoms and
        Herbs with Pasta, 148
    and Basil Pasta Salad, 91
    Blossoms, Ricotta-Stuffed, 94
    Fran's, with Peanut Sauce, 94
    Fresh Zucchini Rellenos, 95
    Grilled, with Fresh Rosemary Butter, 93
    Pancakes, 96
    Pizza, Ten Minute, 96
    Relish, Fran's Blue-Ribbon, 89
    Salad/Pickle, Indonesian, 92
    Stuffed Herbed, 90
    in Tex-Mex Casserole, 33
    with Walnuts, 89

For A Second Batch Of Recipes From Renee Shepherd And Fran Raboff . . .

MORE RECIPES FROM A KITCHEN GARDEN
by Renee Shepherd & Fran Raboff

From the authors of *Recipes from a Kitchen Garden,* we offer this bumper crop of 300 more tasty creations. Featuring a wide range of vegetables, aromatic herbs, and garden specialties such as chiles and edible flowers, this companion to the first volume is again filled with delightful illustrations, sure to capture the imagination and enthusiasm of gardeners and cooks alike.

Grow Your Own Vegetables . . .

LAZY-BED GARDENING by John Jeavons & Carol Cox

This "Quick and Dirty Guide" distills the essentials of biointensive gardening for those who don't have the time or inclination to put in a lot of effort. Based on John Jeavons's classic *How to Grow More Vegetables (than you ever thought possible on less land than you can imagine),* it focuses on simple techniques for getting started on a small, easy to maintain, but highly productive garden.

THE KITCHEN GARDENER'S GUIDE
edited by Donald Berg

Not that long ago, every homemaker depended on a kitchen garden for fresh produce all year round. The time-tested secrets in this book will allow anyone to plan, seed, grow and harvest a bounty for the table.

THE AFTER-DINNER GARDENING BOOK
by Richard W. Langer

A hilarious offbeat guide to using household items (coffee cans, bathtubs, etc.) to grow a steady supply of fresh, interesting produce—from coconuts to pineapples to banana trees—using seeds from food you eat every day. A very different kind of gardening book for the botanically inclined, or for anyone who simply likes a good read!

And Once You've Grown Them . . .

LOST ARTS by Lynn Alley

There was a time when virtually every home cook knew how to cure olives, make flavored vinegars, bake all manner of goodies, and grow herbs for medicinal and culinary uses galore. Lynn Alley has collected a fascinating group of these lost arts—hints, recipes, instruction, and folklore—all of which can be prepared with a minimum of effort using modern, time-saving kitchen equipment.

THE NEW LAUREL'S KITCHEN
by Laurel Robertson, Carol Flinders, & Brian Ruppenthal

Millions of people have enjoyed the wonderful recipes from this delightful cookbook. With its warm tone and lovely art, this new edition contains updated nutritional information and hundreds of healthful dishes.

MOOSEWOOD COOKBOOK by Mollie Katzen

This top-to-bottom revision of our bestselling cookbook adds delicious new recipes and retains all the old favorites, but reflects today's lighter tastes. "One of the most attractive, least dogmatic meatless cookbooks . . . an engaging blend of hand-lettered care and solid food information."

Available from your local bookstore, or call 1-800-841-BOOK for information on how to order directly from the publisher. Write for our free complete catalog of over 500 books, posters and tapes.

🌀 Ten Speed Press, P.O. Box 7123, Berkeley, CA 94707